KAYANG
& ME

This is a powerfully honest story. A story of family, land and identity. At its centre, Kayang Hazel, compassionate, wise and strong. A story to open your heart to.

Sally Morgan

Even before I'd finished *Kayang & Me* I knew the value of it and enjoyed learning and being enriched by both voices. Life stories told in both 'Noongar talk' by Hazel Brown, mixed with the award-winning style of her nephew Kim Scott demonstrate the significant role of oral history in learning about Indigenous Australia and, while presenting a family history, explore not only the complexity but also the evolution of Aboriginal identity and culture nationally.

Anita Heiss

Kim Scott is a descendant of people living along the south coast of Western Australia prior to colonisation, and is proud to be one among those who call themselves Noongar. His writing has won numerous awards and prizes, including two Miles Franklin Literary Awards. Kim's novels include *True Country*, *Benang: from the heart* and *That Deadman Dance*. He is currently Professor of Writing at Curtin University in Western Australia.

Hazel Brown is the senior elder of a large, extended Noongar family. She has worked as a rural labourer, was a member of Western Australia's first Metropolitan Commission of Elders, and is a registered Native Title claimant over part of the south coast of Western Australia.

KIM SCOTT
HAZEL BROWN

KAYANG
& ME

FREMANTLE PRESS
fine independent publishing

For Bob Pirrup Roberts and Fanny Winnery

Wilomin Noongar

I remember when they used to go hunting. Dad used to be late coming back to camp and the boys'd be wondering. I'd say, 'Oh, Pa won't be long.'

They reckoned, 'Oh, Pa mighta got drownded.'

And I'd say, 'No, he'll light a fire directly. When he come over the hill he'll light a fire and he'll show us.' And next thing you see smoke, and then — not long — Dad coming down the slope towards us.

That's how Noongar used to do it. Years ago they used to light fires to let people know where they were, you know.

Grandfather Dongup was bringing cattle up from Hopetoun. He said he saw the smoke those Noongars made, top of the hill, and there musta been a lot of them. They was going for a meeting, exchanging women or something like that I suppose. When he came back, there was no-one.

See, most of 'em travelled from Jerdacuttup, just to go and get killed at Cocanarup.

My name is Hazel Brown. I was born on the ninth of November 1925, at a place called Kendenup. My mother and her first husband, they were working down there. A lot of people used to trap possum you know, for the pelts.

I was born in an old packing shed. Years ago no women had their babies in hospital, you weren't allowed to. They had their babies in the bush.

My mother was Nellie Limestone from Marble Bar; she was born at Lydon station. Her mother was Mary Williams, a full-blood Aboriginal from the Pilbara district. Her father was supposed to have been a white man.

My mother was one of the Stolen Generations. She was sent to the Carrolup Native Settlement — now called Marribank — near Katanning. She was known there as Nellie Limestone, but there were too many Nellies around so they changed her name to Sybil when they made her get married.

She used to run away from there. Jack Cornwall was doing work for a farmer at Boscabel, in the Beaufort River district, and my father was working for him. Jack had a horse and cart, and he used to give the girls a lift to where the men were.

When the white bosses from the settlement went after the young girls they took a black tracker with them, and the policeman in charge of Katanning police station, he went too. Mum and Aunty Anne Morrison were caught, and Dad Yiller and Mum were made to get married. That was in 1920.

My father's name was Freddy Roberts. Yiller was his Aboriginal name. He was born at Jacup, a place between Ravensthorpe and Jerramungup in the Fitzgerald area. He died in Katanning District Hospital in the year 1930, on the thirtieth of November.

My mother had two children by then, and after Fred Yiller died, well me and Lenny were going to be sent to Carrolup Settlement, so Fred Yiller's brother, Fred Tjinjel Roberts, married my mother. That was Noongar way, see. She was accepted into the family, and that meant her husband's brother looked after her when the husband died.

There were three Freds in the family. There was the eldest brother Yiller, and there's Booker, and there's Tjinjel, and they all went by the name of Fred, so there was no one Fred; there was Fred This and Fred That. But my father was Fred Roberts, and that's the name we've been known by, and then I married Harry Brown and that's when I became a Brown.

I spent my early years in the Needilup and Jerramungup districts, and the first language I was taught was Noongar talk. I only ever spoke the language of our people from the south of the state. I was never taught the language of my mother's tribe.

I grew up with my brothers and sister among our father's full-blood relations. When we were young we always kept the laws of our people who were traditional people. We mostly lived in bag camps — you know, like tents made out of old hessian bags and canvas and that — and we slept on rushes or bushes for our beds. We ate the bush food of our people, too.

I was just seven years of age when I was taught to track, snare, hunt and gather food. I was also taught how to use a gun. I shot rabbits, parrots, ducks, and at the age of ten I shot my first kangaroo. My teacher was my father's brother, who became a father to me.

I never had to shoot the possum because I climbed the tree and pulled it out by the legs or tail. We often went hunting for mallee hen nests and if there were eggs in the nest we would always leave one or two for the mothers to look after.

I was taught about the laws and the traditions of the people of our region by my parents and elders. Our people were mostly kept together by Henry Dongup and Waibong Moses. They and the other old people made my second father marry my mother.

My father's father was called Bob Roberts (also known as Pirrup), and his mother was called Monkey, a woman who came from the Ravensthorpe district. My second father was also the son of Pirrup, and his mother was Emily Mudda Dabb.

Most of my grandmother Monkey's family were massacred some time after 1880 by white people at a place called Cocanarup, a few miles from the Ravensthorpe townsite. Some of Granny Emily's people died there too.

My grandfather Pirrup's father was Bobby Roberts, whose family came from the Hunter River, about five miles from Bremer Bay. Great-grandfather Bobby's mother was of the Wilomin people.

Wilo, that's us. We're Wilomin. A long-legged people. Well, we weren't all long-legged, but that's what they called our people. Like, Lenny had the long skinny legs … Me, I got the name Yaakiny, 'cause I was the slow one. Turtle, that's me. They would be quick quick while I'm lagging and I'm coming behind …

*

My name is Kim Scott. Not long-legged at all, I'm following even further behind Aunty Hazel.

My father, Tommy Scott, was the only surviving child to an Aboriginal woman who died when he was ten years old, after which his Aboriginal grandmother continued to raise him until his Scottish father arranged boarding schools and even a succession of stepmothers. He still occasionally saw his grandmother. Sometimes, too, an aunty or uncle looked after him.

When I was a child my father told me to be proud I was 'of Aboriginal descent'. Perhaps it was the silence surrounding his words that made them resonate as they did; I'd certainly heard no such thing anywhere else in my life, certainly not in my reading or schooling. There didn't seem much in the way of empirical evidence to support my father's words. A child, and unable to either calibrate injustice and racism or identify its cause, I sensed the legacy of oppression.

I remember a young man running to my father for help in escaping a family feud, crying that 'they' were gunna get him and chop his legs off. A baby — one among a series of several entrusted to us by a neighbouring elder while the parents were unable to care for them — died after being accidentally placed in a bath of scalding water soon after returning to his home. Peering through the fly-screen, for the first time I saw my mother sobbing uncontrollably.

Most of Aunty Hazel's writing in this book comes from transcriptions of tape-recordings we did together. That method created some difficult decisions for us, most of which could be reduced to the particular problem of how to capture the distinctive nature of her speech while allowing it to be relatively smooth to read on the page. For example, Aunty Hazel says 'Jerrymungup' or 'Jerry' when she's talking about the place most books and maps label 'Jerramungup'. She'll often articulate 'nineteen hundred and twenty-two', not 'nineteen twenty-two', and she says 'coulda', not 'could've'. Generally, we've chosen the variant more common on the printed page: 1922, not 1900-and-22; Jerramungup, not Jerrymungup.

Authentically reproducing Aunty Hazel's sound in print became even more of a problem when she used Noongar language. Partly that's because the English alphabet doesn't do justice to the sounds of Noongar, but also because we've used the spelling and orthography recommended by the Noongar Language and Cultural Centre's 1992 dictionary, and this doesn't fit the south-east dialect as well as it might. The sounds represented by the letters 'b' and 'd' are much more like 'p' and 't', for instance, and there's a greater frequency of middle diphthongs and relatively few vowels at the end of words; the word for water, for instance, is more like 'ka-ip', in contrast to what is usually written as 'kep', or 'kepa' in other dialects.

Mostly, we've opted for compromise in the interests of communicating more widely. We've used very little Noongar language in this book anyway, not only for the above reasons, but because it's a language that's best transmitted orally. You need to listen.

A further problem with putting speech into writing arose when we looked at transcripts of interviews with Aunty Hazel conducted more than twenty years ago, in which she used expressions like 'people of colour' or 'coloured people' more often than the terms 'Noongar' or 'Aboriginal', and makes a distinction between 'half-castes' and 'full-bloods'.

When I read those terms it made me think about how the language we use, and the ways of thinking it encourages, can change over even a relatively short time. I wondered if something of that distinction between 'half-caste' and 'full-blood' was implicit in my father's words when he said 'Aboriginal descent', and whether it also existed in my own thinking as a child. I know I identified with those Aboriginal people who were achieving in the society I knew and felt a part of: the boxer, Lionel Rose, who also recorded country and western songs; Jimmy Little, the musician; a range of Australian Rules footballers like Sydney Jackson, Polly Farmer and Barry Cable.

I gravitated to what I thought might be the literature of 'coloured people', and naively read Kipling's *Kim*, devouring it without being conscious of the identity confusion of its protagonist and the strange cultural appropriation taking place. I remember my father reading a series of novels in a sub-genre typified by one titled *Mandingo*, and although I don't recall ever seeing *Uncle Tom's Cabin* it's plausible that my father — since I, in my innocence, could identify with Kipling's Kim — may even have felt an affinity with Uncle Tom. Well, he may have been an uncle to some, but he was father to me.

I also remember, not long before he died, seeing a copy of *Poor Fellow My Country* opened beside my father's empty chair. I'd guess my father could identify with Prindy, but where was the tribal elder to guide him?

My father and I didn't have a lot of conversations, which is probably why I remember those we did have, like when — at six or seven years old — I came home bruised and bleeding and cursing two other Noongar boys — strangers — I'd clashed with after they'd stolen my younger brother's bicycle. 'Coons,' I was calling them.

My father shut me up. Don't talk that way, he said. People are people. And for the first time he told me to be proud I was 'of Aboriginal descent'.

Perhaps my father's words resonated so strangely simply because, in 1960s south-western Australia, it was hard to articulate pride in Aboriginality. My father wanted me to have something more like a faith, a psychological conviction. It was not something easily put into words. He said to be proud, that was the important thing, but he lacked the vocabulary, didn't have the right stories at hand. It's a continuing problem I think, this struggle to articulate the significance and energy of a specific Indigenous heritage.

In the mid 1960s it was put to me in terms of being proud to be 'of Aboriginal descent' and 'part-Aboriginal', but not much more than ten years later I was a young adult living and working among Aboriginal people of south-western Australia — Noongars — who repeatedly said, 'You can't be bit and bit. What are you, Noongar or wadjela?'

It was a political imperative about the need to commit, to align oneself with either white or black, and I felt compelled to obey. There didn't seem to be any choice, not if I wished to be among Noongars. But even as I winced at the phrase 'Aboriginal descent' and learned more of our shared history, our story of colonisation, I was not always confident of my acceptance by other Noongars.

My father died in his thirties. Young as he was, he was several years older than his mother had been at the time of her death.

I didn't grow up in the bush. There was no traditional upbringing of stories around the camp fire, no earnest transmission of cultural values. The floor of the first house I remember was only partially completed, and my three siblings and I, pretending we were tight-rope walkers, balanced on the floor-joists spanning the soft dirt and rubble half a metre below us.

We moved to a government house on a bitumen street with gutters running down each side, and even though the street came to an end, the slope ran on and on through patchy scrub and past the superphosphate factory, the rubbish tip, the Native Reserve.

Individuals were fined for being on the reserve, and fined for being in town. Their crime was being non-Aboriginal in the one place and Aboriginal in the other, after legislation was refined in the attempt to snare those who — as the frustrated bureaucrat put it — 'run with the hares and hunt with the hounds' and to trip them as they moved to and fro across a dividing legislative line.

My father was mobile that way, always moving.

From the city where he'd reached adulthood, he moved back close to the country of our Noongar ancestors, and worked on the roads as 'leading hand' in a gang of mainly Aboriginal men. Returning home after being away from us for ten days of every fortnight, he usually took us camping. He wanted to be a professional fisherman, and we rattled along the coast in a battered 4WD and trailed nets from a dinghy in the country of our countless ancestors, 'going home' together. We kids helped with the nets, cleaned fish, and even hawked them around the neighbourhood. My mother broke up blocks of ice with the back of an axe, and we carefully layered fish and ice into crates which my father then loaded onto a train bound for the city.

One among other Noongar and wadjela children running barefoot in a suburb a skip, hop and a step from the reserve, I was only ever at the fringe of a community which showed all the signs of being under siege.

I knew my father's mother and grandmother had lived around Ravensthorpe and Hopetoun, two very small towns in the very south of Western Australia. Hopetoun, on the coast, was the port for Ravensthorpe, some fifty kilometres inland, and were it not for an explosion of mining which began in the very late nineteenth century and lasted a decade or so into the twentieth, it would probably never have existed. Hopetoun is a little too exposed for a port; the sealers and whalers and ships of the colonists mostly preferred bays either side of it for the shelter they provide from the persistent southerly winds which chop and toss the sea onto the white beach. As Ravensthorpe and its mines dwindled, so too did Hopetoun.

I was born in the capital city of the state, far away and about sixty years after the proclamation of those southern towns, and returned to Albany, the largest town on the south coast, to do my schooling before moving away again for further education. When I began teaching and working among Noongar people, I only met one or two who knew my grandmother's name. The few who remembered my dad didn't know his family.

Some of my father's relatives were visibly Aboriginal, but lived apart from the wider Noongar community. It was awkward to ask certain questions of them. One such uncle insisted that his mother and her forebears were not from the south-west but, 'South Australia, she was from South Australia.'

So I knew very few members of my extended Indigenous family, and they were either ashamed to admit to their Aboriginality, or — like my father had perhaps been — too diffident to loudly identify themselves as Aboriginal. Maybe they thought the real Aboriginal people were the down-and-outs, the losers. They might have had mostly negative understandings of what it was to be Aboriginal, and less sense of kinship with the local Indigenous community than even I had, courtesy of my father and people we knew.

Clearly, I had very few close relations who identified themselves and were accepted as Noongar. We must originally be from some place else I thought, and not from around those tiny towns of Hopetoun and Ravensthorpe.

Names plucked from a family tree and the knowledge that my father had attended a particular mission school led me to a remote Aboriginal community with which the mission was associated. I applied to be a teacher at the government school there, hoping to connect with Indigenous family with roots in country and community.

I was not successful. The name was coincidental, but the disappointment of not finding the country or people I came from fed my first novel, which I wrote with the lyrics of Midnight Oil's

'Dead Heart' stuck to the wall beside my desk. The chorus of that song is defiant — how we carry the true country in our hearts, and how our ancestry cannot be broken — but I think the novel emerged from the chasm between the affirmation of those lyrics and the title's sorry tale of loss. 'True country' indeed.

Some years later, co-ordinating an Aboriginal bridging course at a local university, I wanted to run the annual 'cultural field trip' in Noongar country, led by Noongar people. Many of the students weren't happy with this, since the alternative was a trip to exotic and warmer destinations, and most thought that there was only 'oppression culture' left in Noongar country — not 'high' culture, not creation stories, language and songs. I worried they were right, but believed that such a course of study in south-western Australia had to acknowledge the primacy of Noongar people and culture. I heard of a family group needing to test the logistics of a 'cultural tourism' enterprise they were developing, and volunteered our group as their clients.

We were not to know it but our guide and elder, Mr Ralph Winmar, was in the last year of his life, and so we were among a privileged few to be properly introduced to the intimacies of his home country, and welcomed with the songs and language of its ancestral spirits.

He sent a group of us to climb the rocky side of that creative spirit, the Waakal — or at least that transformed remnant of it fenced within a small rectangle of the wheat belt somewhere around Quairading and York. On the climb we tasted water running from the wound left by an ancestral Noongar's spear and, standing high on the Waakal's fossilised back, looked out over a tractor describing small futile circles in the paddock below us, and heard the bleating of distant tiny sheep. The breeze in our faces, and the air entering our lungs did not — despite the cleared paddocks and the fences and sheep and tractor — belong to any place known only as 'the wheat belt'.

It seemed true; an old spirit rests in the land and we, its people, are the catalyst of its awakening. It's a potential, a possibility, that still excites me.

I mentioned to one of the elders accompanying us that my Aboriginal family had lived in Ravensthorpe. She said, 'Oh, I hope not, for your sake.' I didn't know what she meant. Someone else suggested I go see Aunty Hazel. They reckoned Hazel Brown knew everyone who'd lived around Ravensthorpe.

Aunty Hazel's genealogical knowledge almost failed her the first time I rang, and back then I didn't realise how rare this was. With only the sound of my voice over the telephone, my surname, and a rough idea of where my family had lived, she nevertheless named my Scottish grandfather's brother and a Noongar woman *he'd* partnered. 'You must be their grandson,' she said.

'No ...'

'Tommy Scott; was he your father then?' she asked.

When I came to visit she held her arms out to me. Small and wiry, she's quite fair-skinned. We had those characteristics in common, anyway. Two fair-skinned and sinewy people, embracing.

People are happy to say of each of us that, well, walking down the street, you wouldn't know ... They look like a wadjela, you wouldn't know they were a Noongar.

Wadjela Noongar was the term Aunty Hazel used when she explained, rather than introduced me, to one of her adult grandchildren. Whiteman Noongar: it's a phrase with subtle increments of meaning which range, depending on tone and context, all the way from 'one of us' to 'one of them'.

Aunty Hazel knew of my youngest brother through her son and

grandson. And yes, of course, she remembered my father. Him and her man Harry Brown used to drink and chase women together. Grinning wryly, she said they thought they were a couple of deadly *bandji* men — meaning sexually promiscuous.

Your father was my cousin, she told me. She remembered him bragging about his Aboriginal relations when he was drinking with a lot of people camping with her family in Borden. Aunty Hazel said he used to be at their camp all the time when he was working on the roads out that way, not long after he'd moved back from the city. When she asked her father Fred Roberts — Pa Tjinjel — who this man's family was, Pa Tjinjel said, 'He's our people, but wait for him to ask.'

My father never did. Too proud, maybe. I think I understand how he wanted others to claim and embrace him. He thought it was enough to have known his grandmother, some uncles and aunts, to have a general awareness of cousins. Perhaps he didn't want to humble himself — or risk rejection. I understand that. He was drinking, he was bragging.

Of course, in other situations it wasn't wise to boast about Noongar family, or even mix with them. It was a crime, and no-one would choose to have the law applied to them the way it did to Noongar people back then.

Aunty Hazel remembers my fair-skinned father among Noongars even though, like herself, he would have been able to move in white society in a way that other Noongars could not, and I guess that gave him an advantage. It's something Aunty Hazel and her brother Uncle Lomas talk about: the difference between being a Noongar with white skin and one with black skin. Not because of anything inherent, but because people treat you according to the degree to which you are recognisably 'Aboriginal'. That was true in the past, and still is.

Why didn't Pa Tjinjel offer the information? I guess because being asked was an acknowledgement of his authority, and a way of paying respect to him. He probably knew fair-skinned Noongars who'd turned their backs on their families and accepted the imperatives of white law.

Aunty Hazel seemed pleased I'd come to her now.

I'd visit, and she'd be raking the dry yard of her suburban government house, or hanging out laundry, or solving some family problem. For most of the time we spent on this manuscript two of her adult grandchildren — Milana and Clinton — lived with her. Both are schizophrenics. There were great-grandchildren in the house too, including little Brayton, whose frail heart was expected to sustain him for only a few years more.

When Aunty Hazel was seventy-five years old she heard that a grand-daughter, Lindley, had left her violent partner and was in a hospital in New South Wales, and that welfare had taken the children. Aunty Hazel organised funding and flew across the continent to bring mother and children back, even though it meant more people to care for in her little home.

An adult nephew, Buddy, injured in a collision between a truck and his motorcycle, was in her care for the last twenty-four years of his life. His was one of the first Noongar funerals I attended as family and, even then, I had to be introduced to almost everyone.

I remember suggesting to Aunty Hazel that she record the sorts of things she knew — the genealogies, the language, the sites and stories and history.

'Go on then,' she said.

I think she was enjoying some of the attention *Benang* was receiving, and especially the gossip about whose family I belonged to.

Recounting her recent visit to an office of Indigenous bureaucracy she suddenly said, 'You know, some of them there don't reckon you're Noongar,' and burst into laughter. I was taken by surprise, and couldn't see that it was something to laugh about. She continued leafing through the pages of a transcript I'd returned to her and then suddenly looked up and asked if I thought we could make a book together.

'We can try,' I said.

I'd often wedge a tape-recorder between us wherever we sat; it might be in the living room among various heaps of fresh laundry, an electric bar heater glowing in the winter gloom. Other times we sat out in the sun on a bush-timber bench her son Eric had built. There were nearly always children about, and on the tapes their conversation and games often accompany our voices.

Sometimes, other visitors looked at me twice, clearly thinking 'Who? Wadjela?' but once I was introduced the tension dissipated.

Aunty Hazel is quite deaf, and I'd have to shout to be heard. Even then she closely watched my face as I spoke. So mostly I'd listen, nod, gesture. Sometimes we'd study notes I'd written up, diagrams and drawings, photographs and bits of books. Occasionally, someone listening would want to join in.

What did she want to talk about? Transcribing her voice, I noticed there were only passing references to things which are ordinarily regarded as momentous in an individual's life: cancer, a nervous breakdown, the time her lung haemorrhaged as she stepped from the train after having spent months away so that she only had time to kiss the family before returning to the hospital.

It wasn't these things she wanted to talk about.

Her grandson Ryan Brown told me how she had once called him over to her when he was whingeing about something or other and, lifting the edge of her shirt, told him to feel the side of her chest. His hand entered a gaping hole in her ribcage where her ribs had been removed. Cancer. Decades ago.

Get over it, she was saying. No point feeling sorry for yourself.

What did she want to talk about?

We looked at photographs, leafed through old 'Native Welfare' files, and I remember her turning away in disappointment and disgust at the record of my ancestor, Harriette Coleman, telling the police she was 'quarter-caste' not 'half-caste'. No self-respecting Noongar would ever do such a thing, so they say, and I felt ashamed of her lie. But now, knowing her audience and the consequences of being classified as 'Aboriginal' at that time, I understand the old lady's words.

It's the sort of behaviour that makes Aunty Hazel angry, but she reacted very differently to some ancestral Noongar names I'd fished from the archives. I offered, 'Wongin, or was it Wonyin?' Aunty Hazel sat up straight. 'Pinyan' gave her another injection of energy. And when I said, 'Winnery. Fanny Winnery,' she laughed out loud, and exclaimed, 'Granny Winnery!'

'Winnery,' she said, 'that's a Hunter River name. That's from the head of the Hunter River. Wilomin people.'

*

Old great-great-grandmother's old father used to shout like a curlew, and disguise himself to look like a curlew. And that's why that family called themselves Wilomin. Wilo, that means curlew, see? And actually they're a very shy bird. You'll hear them, but you'll very seldom see 'em. Unless you're very quiet. Very, very quiet.

Wilo, they got long legs, and there's only a bit of a bird on top, and they have this long neck, and they can flatten themselves down just like a piece of dry stick and they'll never move. Even if you're watching them, they'll shut their eyes and you'll think they're a piece of rock.

Mrs Hassell — *My Dusky Friends*, you read that, unna? — called our people 'Wheelman'. 'Wilamen,' some say.

But we Wilomin.

Wilomin people used to communicate between Bremer and bottom side of Quaalup down that side, and they used to go to Bremer and they used to go to Doubtful Island, 'cause they travel around everywhere, see. And some of these people, they go down there and mix with other mob, see? They were friendly tribe, and that's where the wilo was, up the river, see?

But it's a funny thing Kim, years ago, 1947, there was Dad, myself, and his brother Malcolm, my husband Harry Brown, one of my cousins — Rita Dempster's brother Adrian Allen — and we had another boy with us, Dad's sister's grandson, Tommy Woods. We had a green ute, and it belonged to my old man. Well, Daddy said, 'Let's go up the Hunter River,' 'cause Harry had shotguns. See, go and shoot some ducks, 'cause plenty of ducks up there, the Hunter River.

We went so far, and then because the motor was low Harry was frightened to go any further because the bushes might pull the wires out.

'All right, leave the motor here.'

Harry had the shotgun and Uncle Malcolm had the .22, and we were gunna go for ducks, see.

Anyways, we got right in the swamp, freshwater, got right up there close, and just before we get towards where the old camps were, Daddy said, 'You gotta stop here now, and make a fire. You gotta make smoke and let 'em know that you're coming.'

So he cleared the ground and then he got a little bit of dry grass and he dug a hole and he lit a fire. He had to be very careful, 'cause it was summertime and we didn't have any water.

The fire burned up and he chucked some green bushes on; and then the smoke, see. Soon as the smoke went up … well, you shoulda heard the curlews, boy. Hear them singing out. They're singing out over there, and then on this side. All around us.

Weeee … Weeeee … Wilo wilo wilo.

And you know when they make a noise, and you're not used to it, that wilo cry can be very frightening.

I was amazed you know. We just stood there and looked at one another. How they made a noise, all around us.

Well, we looked at one another. Me and Tommy, we were scared. Shivers went up and down my back.

Daddy said, 'That's it, you're right. That's the Wilomin people; they're letting us know. We're right now.' And he just hit the two sticks together like that, and no more.

We heard 'em, but we didn't see one.

That's something I'll always remember, you know. When we heard them all around us. About eleven o'clock. It was just like a chorus, and it was most frightening.

They're letting us know that they know you're here. Like that old song, '*Wilo wang mia wang wo da badin kabin ngayn* …' You heard that one? The curlew sound, you know, 'I wonder is it for me?' Like, lotta Noongars they think, oh, death bird, you know. But not us. Not we Wilomin. They speak to us.

But when we were kids we were dead scared, to hear them

in the night, you know. When we were living out in the bush, if we heard 'em, you just crawl in and pull the blanket over your head and you froze. You froze, you never moved.

*

It transfixed me, this story of spirits calling.

A Noongar name at the beginning of a sequence of English ones had enabled Aunty Hazel to connect me to a specific place on the south coast, not so far, as it happened, from Ravensthorpe and Hopetoun.

Wilomin Noongar. What does that mean?

Aunty Hazel reckons the wilo can completely camouflage itself. It closes its eyes and just lies there, motionless. You only see it when its eyes open.

An endangered species along the south coast, the wilo lays its eggs in the sand. As foolish as an artist, I thought; as vulnerable as someone 'of Aboriginal descent' forsaking camouflage and, with his eyes open, asking after his Aboriginal family.

My family didn't bequeath me a rich oral history, quite the contrary, but there was one story of a boy and his mother camped past the edge of the town of Ravensthorpe, sitting around the fire and hearing the curlews calling.

Wilo.

The boy asked the woman why those birds were doing that, making such a scary sound. She told him those wilo had seen him slouching and dragging his feet as he walked home from school, and they were jeering at him. She said he should remember to hold his head up. Walk like them, perhaps she meant, like a wading bird; deliberate, fastidious, proud. Don't slump like the defeated or dead, but have the poise of those surrounded by risk and habitually wary.

Aunty Hazel translated Wilomin as 'curlew-like', the curlew people; it's how she and her brothers and sister grew up thinking of themselves. They weren't familiar with other names, or the descriptions and boundaries that anthropologists and historians use to describe people of the region. Oh, they've since come to know something of the writings of Ethel Hassell, a member of one of the pioneering families of the region. And even as a child Aunty Hazel had heard of Daisy Bates, but not the names and descriptions Bates gave of Noongars. 'Kurin,' Bates says of those in the region Aunty Hazel calls traditional country, but then Bates also uses the name 'Wilu-wuk' — a reference to people associated with the curlew — and is rather vague about the area they inhabit. Norman Tindale, who gathered his information in the 1930s and seems to be accorded pre-eminent authority these days because of the extent of his documentation and its use in Native Title forums, labels the peoples of the approximate area discussed by Aunty Hazel as variously Koreng, Wudjari and Wiilman. Tindale was so confident of his demarcations that he identified a 'Boundary Rock'.

Different peoples? The same? Such things as dialects of a common language, ties formed by trade and intermarriage, 'skin' groupings, 'totems' and 'moieties' all imply various and shifting groupings, as do the differing experiences of colonisation within and between the missions, 'settlements', reserves, country towns and cities. Depending upon circumstances and temperament, there's a range of responses available along a shifting continuum of accommodation and adaptation, resistance and assimilation …

Can any map, any one word, any one authority or committee do more than approximate who were, and are, the people indigenous to a particular region?

Before meeting Aunty Hazel I'd followed a trail through the archives — a trail remarkable merely for its existence considering the decades when the births of Noongars, even those with white fathers, were rarely recorded. The trail led to an area of the south-east coast of Western Australia where my Indigenous ancestors had lived. The ocean runs along one edge of that country, and at other boundaries it blurs into country that the archives and political maps, with their love of demarcation and frontiers, cannot always be precise about. What sub-group of Noongar is this, I wondered. Or is it Ngadju, even Mirning, territory?

Researching *Benang*, I was also looking into family history, and one phrase kept appearing: 'the first white man born' in such and such a place. It was in countless local histories, and in my notes I reduced it to the ugly initials, FWMB.

A book written by an early twentieth-century authority on Aboriginal matters — A O Neville — offered a visual variation on FWMB in a photograph of three figures captioned:

> *Three generations (reading from Right to Left). 1. Half-blood — (Irish Australian father; full-blood Aboriginal Mother). 2. Quadroon Daughter — (Father Australian born of Scottish parents; Mother No. 1). 3. Octaroon Grandson — (Father Australian of Irish descent; Mother No. 2).*

It could almost be a family photograph, but what family would describe itself that way?

Perversely, the phrase 'first white man born' energised me. As alienating and hostile as the words were, I was familiar with the language.

I detected another recurring phrase: 'the last full blood aborigine'.

Yes, there it was in *Pioneers of the Ravensthorpe and District,* and again in Ravensthorpe and Hopetoun's *Visitor Map and Information Guide*: 'The last full blood aborigine of the area, Geordie, died in 1944.'

The 'last full blood aborigine': LFBA.

FWMB, LFBA: the two sets of initials littered my notes. They seemed to insist on a boundary, a demarcation; the end of an old story, the beginning of a new one — and the concept of race was at the centre of it.

I must have dozed off in the archives, fallen like a mote of dust among the loops and wriggles on dusty parchment, because I remember feeling as if I had just surfaced and — blinking, looking around with watery eyes, suddenly too warm and solid in the stuffy airconditioning — wondering where I was.

Who I was.

'The first white man born?'

There's a poem by Ted Hughes — 'The Thought Fox' — which I read as about the act of creation, and in which writing is characterised as akin to hunting; an intuitive tracking and seizing.

Another poet, Charles Boyle, writes:

> What do I know about fishing? Only the lure
> Of its skills: patience and cunning; the arcane lore
> Of tackle and rod, unravelling knots in the tangled net;
> The practice of solitude …

Perhaps I go too far, reading such words as a metaphor for writing, but beginning this book with Aunty Hazel I had only a vague idea of what lay within the language and stories she offered, and even less of what it might become. Was I patient? Perhaps. Solitary? Yes, in a way. Cunning?

I'd collected fossilised phrases like 'first white man born', and tossed them back into the sea of the archives in the hope of somehow making a firmer footing for myself. But with Aunty Hazel I stood on the sandy shore of my Indigenous heritage, and sensed something substantial and sustaining waiting for me to grasp, and yet the only means I had to do so was this laying out of words upon a page.

If writing is indeed comparable to hunting or fishing, then Aunty Hazel was showing me another way to go about it.

*

At certain times of the year the Noongar people used to go down and do their fishing. My little brother, Uncle Cedric, knew a lot about all this.

Groper fishing is more of a men's thing. Very, very sacred. Very, very quiet. Top skills for that, even with a line. If the groper sees you, you don't see him anymore. He's cleverer than the Noongar. Unless you crush and break up crabs to feed him and bring him back. If he's really hungry he'll come back. But, in our way, you can learn that.

A pack of gropers, a little more than twenty-five — that's the whole family. You catch them out, you got no more. So you catch what you need, and you leave the rest, specially the old fellas. Don't take more than one or two each.

Songs for that, for groper.

They used to sing old songs, not only for groper, for salmon too. Old Dongup and his brother old Winmir, they went and painted up and the other fellas made a fire, you know.

You light a fire on the beach and sing out boy — porpoise'll chase the salmon right into you. Hit the stick and sing like a porpoise, talk and shout like a porpoise, and they'll chase all the salmon right in, and salmon, to get away, salmon'll jump right out of the water.

Porpoise, dolphins, don't matter what you call 'em, Noongar'll tell you what they do, they bring the salmon round, bring 'em round like dogs. The old fellas just sat back and whistled, threw the fire up, tapped the water ...

The two old boys standing there, they speared two or three salmon, 'cause them two old spearmen, they two old champions. Dongup and Winmir. We had a good feed of salmon from them.

That was happening for thousands of years, down our way. That was always handed down.

It happened at certain times of the year and the Noongars knew this, and they'd walk miles to get a feed of salmon. Fish that beach themselves. As well as feeding the young porpoise or dolphin, they were happy feeding themselves as well. That's the Noongars.

People still do it. At certain times of the year.

We were down there one year, at Cape Riche, when Eric was small and Buddy, too. It was in February, when the salmon season started, and you know what? I never seen so many dolphins!

There was me and Mrs Kunyo, and her two nieces and a few of my kids, and we watching for salmon. The boys had already taken one load away, and we were sitting down watching for more. Was a lovely afternoon too, oh about two o'clock, and it really wasn't that hot. The sea was just like glass you know, so calm.

And the next minute we see all these black things in the

water. Couldn't believe it, I was rubbing my eyes. 'What these things all coming?' and the next thing you see this big brown patch, that's all the salmon coming … and these porpoises coming from everywhere. The water was teeming with 'em, 'cause they were following the salmon in.

Well, Cedric — my brother, you know, Uncle Chubbo — he was sitting the other side of me. Cedric reckoned, 'Oh, there's hundreds.' I'm sure there were hundreds. And the salmon were just jumping out of the water, they was that frightened, so many of them coming behind.

Well, they just come straight in like that. And, oh, too many. They weren't eating them, just chasing them. They had them salmon, and the salmon would go underneath, darting and leaping to get away from the porpoises.

Ngari, that's salmon.

And whales, there's songs for them too. Grandfather, old fellas, used to sing 'em. I never seen 'em do it, but they told me. And I heard 'em sing.

Whales. *Mamang*.

Whales come in close sometimes, you seen that, unna? Right next to the rocks. Like at Albany now, and Point Anne too. Well one old Noongar, he jumped onto one, and went like inside it. Slipped inside it like Jonah, unna? Like Jonah in the Bible musta done.

But the Noongar knew what he was doing, he *wanted* to be there, see. It wasn't an accident. Like he sung it to him and, well, not grabbed — can't say he grabbed it — but he controlled it, you know, he controlled the whale.

They dived, deep, deep; musta been sorta quiet and dark,

and the Noongar singing, singing this song to the whale and listening to its blood, its heart. They used to sing it, old fellas, not really to us, but for themselves see. I can't remember it, the song, but I remember dreaming it once, woke up ready to sing, but … gone now.

Anyway, Noongar wanted it to take him, carry him Albany way, down there somewhere, lo-o-o-ng way from where he was.

When it come up, like every now and then it'd come up to the surface, and … he was inside the whale, looking out when it come to the surface, you know. Like he *was* the whale … see ocean everywhere, sun, birds maybe, and bubbles when they dived again.

He sung … they used to sing the song. I think he met up with some womans, got 'em *boodjari*, brought 'em back this way to his family.

I can't remember, and I never said that one since … oh, long time.

Sad, that I can't. Dreamt it once, that song; woke up with it in my head, but it went away again.

'On the authority of our native'

When she was a young girl, Aunty Hazel told me, her old people used to visit Granny Winnery all the time and once, she remembered, they came back from Ravensthorpe with a horse. It was a good horse, too. They were excited and happy to have seen Granny Winnery.

Aunty Hazel was told that Granny Winnery was her grandfather Pirrup's sister. She must've been the daughter of old Bobby Roberts, she told me. We don't know his Noongar name; we only know the name the police gave him. Old Bobby worked with the police, Aunty Hazel said, and he went with the explorers.

I went looking for Bobby Roberts in the archives and found a trace of him in John Septimus Roe's expedition journals.

J S Roe was the Swan River Colony's first surveyor-general and remained in that position until 1870 when the colony moved to representative government and he retired. One of the colony's official elite, his political position and his networks made him especially influential in opening the country to pastoral interests.

Roe mentions 'Bob' in the account of his 1849 expedition along the south coast of Western Australia:

> ... *The native lad Souper who accompanied me from York, I regret being obliged to leave here, as he is badly afflicted with Hernia of some standing, and would consequently only embarrass my movements, I have succeeded in engaging in his stead an intelligent native lad of this district, known as 'Bob,' from whom I expect to derive valuable information as to the nature of the country as far as it is known to him.*

Roe wrote this from Cape Riche — a more protected landing than Hopetoun — where he was the guest of a Mr George Cheyne. Cheyne had arrived in Albany in 1831 when the site — until then a British military camp intended to discourage French colonial interest — became an avaricious outpost of empire.

Prior to this, interaction between Noongar and visitors to the area had been limited and various. As elsewhere in Australia, sealers were notorious for killing men and stealing women and girls. There was, however, also contact of a more positive nature. In 1791 George Vancouver left gifts for the absent Noongars as payment for the timber and water he'd taken aboard his ship. Noongars exchanged materials with Matthew Flinders' party in 1801, and with Phillip Parker King some decades later. Dumont Durville briefly established an observatory, and Noongars went aboard his ship.

When Major Lockyer arrived at Albany in 1826 to establish a military camp and a claim on the land in the face of French interest he was openly greeted by Noongar people. When his men were attacked a couple of days later Lockyer realised it was a form of payback for atrocities recently committed by sealers and he prevented retaliation. Perhaps his wisdom helped the Noongar see that not all white people were the same.

The British military unit gave no sign of stealing Noongar territory; they had merely camped within it. The relationship between them and the Noongar community was amicable, and one individual especially — Mokare — developed a remarkable rapport with some of the officials and soldiers.

Secure in his own land, Mokare was confident and generous. He visited the soldiers, showed them around, helped them out. He and his people traded goods with them and made other exchanges.

Once, when someone entered the room in the barracks where Mokare and his brothers were in conversation with some of the soldiers, Mokare sang a line from something he'd heard the soldiers singing: 'Oh where have you been all the day?' Witty, even post-modern of him, the anecdote also hints at the importance he attached to knowing people by their songs, their sound.

Other south-coast Noongars showed similar social confidence. On a visit to the Swan River Colony, a small group of them attended an afternoon piano recital. A colonial diarist reports their delight with the concert, and that they reciprocated with a dance. I imagine them settling into armchairs in their kangaroo skin cloaks as the piano music cascades over them. Sipping tea, even. They were people confident about cross-cultural exchange, and alive to potential and possibility.

Yet another Noongar of those days, Yagan — usually remembered as a resistance warrior betrayed by those white people he regarded as friends, and whose body was beheaded and skinned for the tribal markings so that a macabre trophy might be sent to England — is reported attending an amateur piano recital in the early years of the colony of Perth. Not just a defeated warrior, he was charming and curious, self-assured and accommodating.

I'm drawn to such accounts which reveal the mental acuity bequeathed by a culture, and its adaptability. The journals of Bishop Salvadore at New Norcia Mission, for instance, describe how rapidly certain young Noongars learned the (Spanish) alphabet. Demonstrating a mastery of reading and of making the smallest of marks upon the earth's surface, they marked the letters in the sand in both upper case and lower case, and then, for good measure, backwards. How easily they should have been able to move into this medium we're sharing now.

Salvadore also expresses amazement at how quickly a young Noongar masters the sextant, and — by way of contrast — his frustration with how long another student, an adult sailor, was taking.

The situation of Mokare's people changed as of 1830, when Albany came under the control of the Swan River Colony and the imperatives that motivated it. The military garrison at Albany hadn't competed for resources; nor had it excluded Noongars from their own land, or insist they be enslaved.

In 1831 George Cheyne arrived in Albany to 'take up land.' So soon after the coexistence of soldiers and Noongar, what was the nature of his relationship with Noongars, the original and actual owners of that land?

> ... at that time although we were on friendly terms with the natives they were unacquainted with our habits and they considered they had as good a right to enter our huts as we had ourselves, and in every hut in the settlement were the natives occasionally found so numerous as almost to exclude ourselves, and I was the first settler who made a stand against it ...
>
> I had frequently to use coercive measures to maintain

my rights and during my temporary absences from my hut,
Mrs Cheyne had several unpleasant encounters with
natives. Under the circumstances it must be evident that I
could not leave my wife and property unprotected to go in
search of land.

Coercive measures? Cheyne was one of many requesting military outposts, but I doubt he wanted them modelled on Albany's first military garrison. Cheyne made plans to bring fifty labourers and tradesmen from Scotland and, around 1840, having sold some of his property to the newly arrived Captain J Hassell, he moved east to Cape Riche and made it the centre of sheep-farming and sandal-wood-cutting enterprises which followed the rivers inland. Cape Riche also became the port of call for the many whalers and sealers working the coast. Bay whaling was booming in the 1840s, and the seamen's reliance on rum made them a disruptive presence in the official port of Albany. Cheyne, however, was not a man to be intimidated by drunks. He knew how to be coercive.

Some Noongars joined the whaling parties. In fact, the governor-resident in Albany complained he couldn't even find, let alone coerce, Noongars to track down some 'sheep stealers' because so many had taken the option of working for the whalers. Obviously, with whalers, government officials and pastoralists competing for their labour, Noongars had plenty of options. The pastoralist Captain J Hassell refused to release one of 'his' Noongar workers for police tracking duties, despite official protests, because the man helped him maintain a stable relationship with local Noongars.

Noongars weren't only used as labourers or trackers, and some Noongars were more 'useful' than others. A shepherd at Hassell's Kendenup station was surrounded and threatened with spears, and later testified that his saviour was a:

*... native (who) came up to me calling himself Harrington
the soldier's boy. He took me by the hand, he spoke to the
others, they unshipped their spears and followed me no
further. I shall always think he saved my life ...*

Of course there was violent conflict between Noongars and the
new arrivals, but there must always have been another dimension
too, and the possibility of alliances beyond those of skin colour or
race. The sophisticated and cosmopolitan Mokare had both British
and French friends. 'Harrington the soldier's boy' intervened out of a
sense of compassion, justice, and even kindredness.

So when surveyor-general J S Roe departed Cape Riche with
'our Bob' as his guide, and travelled as far as the Russell Ranges, just
north-east of Esperance, they had time to impress one another.
Despite the power relationship writers tend to impose upon their
subjects, Bobby Roberts is no dumb, silent presence in Roe's journal.
He's clearly an important link not only to the country they are
'exploring' but also to its other inhabitants:

*While at the camp, a Cape Riche native known as 'Bob',
who had been engaged to form one of our party to the
eastward, was visited by several of his friends from Doubtful
Island Bay, and other parts, including two who had walked
with him from what he represented to be the
neighbourhood of Middle Island; but as I could gather from
them nothing more as to the nature of the interior country
than 'Bob' himself was able to communicate, I did not ...
engage the proffered services ...*

Aunty Hazel's great-grandfather Bobby Roberts' relationship with
other Indigenous inhabitants is not always so intimate. Further inland,

he seems to align himself more with his white companions than with Indigenous strangers. Once they come upon a hastily deserted camp; banksia flowers — gathered for their nectar — were heaped in bark and wooden containers beside a crackling fire, but:

> ... nor could they be induced by loud calls and invitations of our native to return and give us an interview. We therefore placed some biscuit in their baskets, left everything as we found it and proceeded on our way, Bob being divided in opinion that they would either have taken us for devils and would never venture near the spot again, or that they were concealed at the time within a very few yards of it.

So appreciative is Roe of his guide's skill in acquiring and preparing food that his journal sometimes sounds like a restaurant review. 'Excellent eating,' he exclaims after dining on groper, and continues:

> Some wild ducks and duck eggs were also added to our larder, the nest being found among the low bushes from 100 to 300 yards back from the river bank.

On another occasion he writes:

> ... (we) moved away to where Bob remembered to have drank fresh water from a well amongst good feed for the horses. In one mile E. by N. we reached it, and were offered another proof of the unerring memory and instinctive sagacity of the aboriginal native ...

And again:

> *Our native said good water was always procurable here by*
> *scratching a small hole in the sand ...*

Given the values of the time, Roe's condescending tone is not surprising, but over the course of the journal the relationship between the surveyor-general and his guide shifts, as is revealed in phrases like:

> *I deferred to the native's judgement ...*
> *On the authority of our native ...*
> *I learned from our native ... this changed my intention ...*
> *and induced me to proceed next day in the opposite*
> *direction.*

By the time they return to Cape Riche, Roe's dependence upon his guide is undeniable. After a few days recovery Roe proposed to set off on their journey back to Perth via Albany, but:

> *It was then found that our native had become tired of the*
> *service on which he had been engaged, and had gone to*
> *rejoin his tribe. Finding it impossible to replace him without*
> *much loss of time, I had to abandon my intentions of taking*
> *a new route to the Westward and through the middle of the*
> *Stirling Ranges, as all the parties agreed in assuring me that*
> *fresh water was then extremely scarce along that line, and*
> *could only be found by the aid of a native.*

But perhaps not just any 'native' would do? Roe — despite the bias of the time — seems to have been particularly impressed by our ancestor, as was clearly shown when they came across a large section of dunes on their way back to Cape Riche.

The clean lines and sharp edges of these huge undulating 'blow-outs' look quite beautiful from a distance, and the windblown sand seems almost like smoke or mist surrounding them. Up close it's different: harsh and dry, and the stinging sand whips at your skin and hair.

Shortly before reaching the dunes Roe's journal offers, as his own wisdom, what he had learned from his guide:

> Fresh water is always to be found among sand hills of the sea coast abreast, by scraping a small hole in the sand …

And then we come to the dunes:

> The entire 'sand patch' was in motion and enveloped in a thick cloud of sand, moving along with as much facility as smoke, and gaining only fresh impetus by the perpendicular resistance it frequently encountered. To move at all amongst these animated sandheaps with our loaded horses seemed at first a proceeding of rather doubtful issue, on account of the fancied quicksands, but on Bob's assurance it was a safe road, always used by the black fellows to avoid the adjoining rocky scrubby country, we advanced into it, and found the footing tolerably firm throughout its whole extent of three or four miles …
>
> While traversing that part of this dreary waste which borders on the sea-coast, we came suddenly upon the skeleton of a human being … Our native immediately explained they were the remains of one of three seamen who had quitted a Hobart Town whaler some 18 months ago in the vicinity of Middle Island for the purpose of walking to Albany …

> *The natives seemed to have been fully aware of the death … and ascribe it to actual starvation and exhaustion, disclaiming most strongly having used any personal violence, but on the contrary, having endeavoured to assist the only one of them they saw before his death, who had, however, through fear or distrust invariably pointed his gun when any of the natives offered to approach him. The unfortunate man now before us was said to be one of them …*

Roe and his group place the body under a cairn of stones, reflecting that soon it will be covered in sand and become fossilised bones. The incident has disturbed them, and they continue:

> *… remarking on the sad spectacle we had just witnessed, having in all probability been occasioned chiefly by want of water, which was everywhere to be had in abundance within a stones throw, by scratching a small hole in the sand.*

I suspect that the repetition of what he'd learned from his guide helps Roe distance himself from the victim. It comforts him, and also suggests how significant an impression his 'native' guide has made.

Roe makes it clear that Bob was more than just a navigation aid, more than merely of assistance in finding food and water, or in liaison with the land's inhabitants. At one stage the expedition party became excited at the country's potential for coalmining:

> *Bob assured me it was not the spot in which his friends had told him coal was to be found …*
>
> *… (we) reached the system of waters belonging to the river on whose estuary our native supposed we should find surface coal …*

> *The Inlet which received this river, being that on which our native had been informed a French Whaling ship had procured coal for use ...*

Excited at the prospect of such mineral resources, Roe also wanted to find good pastoral country. Again, his 'native boy' leads him:

> *I maintained a westerly course for the purpose of striking a river which Bob said we should encounter on the east side of East Mount Barren, and on which he reported good grass.*
>
> *... we encamped at 4 o'clock in the midst of luxuriant grass, in a valley half a mile wide, through which was winding in a very torturous course the river which 'Bob' had described to us.*
>
> *On the authority of our native, this main branch comes from Jeer-a-mung-up, where we had such good country on the 22nd October last, 30 miles to the W. by N. the whole of which space he also said was well grassed and fit for good stock runs ...*

Roe altered his route back to the capital city when Bob couldn't be found, and assumed it was because his guide had returned to the comfort zone of his family and was tired of the work. Perhaps, however, that was not the case, because in the following days Roe passed a number of Hassell's stations where people were preparing to leave. Mr Hassell was 'transferring his principal station to the good country we had discovered ... at Jeeramungup on the Fitzgerald.'

Hassell had obviously received good information.

Most sources suggest it was a botanist, or even a sandalwood cutter who alerted Hassell to where the best grazing land was but, according to Aunty Hazel, it was Bobby Roberts who showed him where he and his sheep might prosper.

In a letter dated 16 January 1849 — while Roe was still making his way from Cape Riche to Perth — Hassell comments that he'd seen surveyor-general Roe's horse tracks at 'Jer-ra-mung-up'.

We reckon Bobby Roberts pointed those out to him, too.

Consider: Bobby Roberts helping the surveyor-general find his way; Bobby Roberts leading the pastoralist to good grazing land and pointing out the tracks of the explorer; Mokare singing the Scottish air; the Noongar intervening to rescue the shepherd ... each a manifestation of a confident and generous culture. In retrospect we might argue that its individuals lacked ruthless political acumen, but nevertheless — as the evidence of a rural labourer of the time indicates — they were more than capable of strategic thinking:

> ... *The natives were making smokes all the way down to the coast, which I understand to be calling the natives together. The three men who took my sheep are Jerrymumup and his son Bobby, and Bulliah, a very large native ...*
>
> ... *a native boy came to me in the bush and sat himself down alongside of me, and while he was eating some bread I had given him I got up to look at my sheep which were feeding on a hill, and on my return I missed the native and he must have taken the bag in which my ammunition was, as the bag was gone; in ten minutes after I missed the boy I saw about 12 or 14 natives going away with a mob of sheep, and I pursued the natives and told them to let the sheep alone and return to the flock; I was about 50 yds from them and 8 of them turning dared me*

to come any nearer, and then I returned to the remainder
of my flock ...

('Outrage by the Natives', *Perth Gazette*, 4 January 1850)

The guile of the militarily under-equipped Noongars makes it
seem almost a game, but games have agreed rules and boundaries,
and the situation was obviously too intense and fluid for any such
consensus to be possible:

> Mc'Donald, who was standing on the hill, called to the natives,
> 'If you spear that man I will shoot you.' On this the natives
> drew off from me; nothing more occurred that day, but the
> next morning we counted over the sheep twice and found
> there were 22 gone, and I asked Mc'Donald where the
> natives encamped and he said on the plain about a quarter
> mile off in scrub; and he (Mc'Donald) went on the upper side
> of the plain and I went the lower side, to see if we could
> recover any of the sheep, and we came up to the camps and
> as soon as the natives saw us they approached towards us
> with their spears shipped, and I said to a man, the headman
> of the tribe, called Jerrymumup, 'What have you done with
> my sheep.' And he said, 'Far away men take the sheep,'
> meaning men from another country. During the time I was
> talking with the natives their women made off as quick as
> possible, but I pursued them so close that one woman had to
> leave her bag and run, and I recognised her to be
> Jerrymumup's woman, I took the bag up and found in it 30 or
> 40 lbs of sheep fat, and I took the bag away from the camps
> and laid it down by a tree, intending to take it home with me,
> and went to look for my sheep, and so did Mc'Donald: when
> we returned the bag had been taken away ...

Of course, this is a caricature of frontier conflict, which was often unjust and violent out of all proportion. Noongars outnumbered the colonisers in the early years on the south coast of Western Australia, and even those who — like Hassell — had been in Tasmania must have understood the need for more sophisticated techniques than open violence. And some Noongars, for various reasons, were prepared to forge alliances with the colonisers; to also be strategic.

'Our' Bobby Roberts, who helped Roe and Hassell, was one of them.

I was startled — shocked — when Aunty Hazel passed a photograph to me and said, 'That's Bobby Roberts, at the end, with the rifle.'

That's what my great-grandfather looked like. Bobby Roberts.

That's his brother. This is all his family, which he brought in from Jerramungup. Bringing 'em into Bremer now see, put 'em on a boat. That's how they all got sent away to Rottnest Island.

Old Bobby did six months in jail for stealing, himself.

These ones here, they must've been related to the Dabb family. The small ones, because the Dabbs were only very small people.

I remember once, Daddy and Uncle Bob having a row, and Uncle Bob taking up with these other fellas. Well, Daddy said to him, 'You got the right name, boy, because you're Bob all right. They should have called us traitors.'

Dad always said they should've called old Bobby a traitor because he turned against Noongar people. He worked against

Noongar people because he knew that the only way he could survive and was guaranteed to be looked after was if he put his hands in the white man's pocket.

A lot of people mightn't like the truth, but this doesn't concern anybody else. This only concerns our people. You got my permission to do it, write it down. Put it in a book. You woulda had Cedric and Lenny's permission to do it, too.

Old Bobby Roberts, he had the privilege of harming his own people with the white man's say-so.

People are going to hear it. We're gunna write it all out, and you're putting it in the book.

There's a lot more stories that should be told, and they're gunna be told. There's a lot of things that've been left unsaid. Too many years now, half-caste people and white people been covering things up. A lot of things. Now we got a chance, we can bring it all out in the open.

I hate the white man who put the gun in my grandfather's hands, so they could get control over Noongars, and gave him the chains, so he could chain them up.

And white people are still doing that today, like with ATSIC and their black bureaucracy.

He was happy, they gave him leggings. But they weren't even proper leggings, only half of one leg, but he was too silly to know that.

He used to work from Bremer and out to Jerramungup, and from Jerramungup he used to go to Ravensthorpe and bring the prisoners back.

*

Aunty Hazel showed me the photograph, believing it to be of her great-grandfather with other Noongar people in chains, although I later found one identical to it in the archives among a series taken in a different part of Western Australia. So it may in fact not be our ancestor, although Aunty Hazel says her grandfather, old Bobby's son, worked with the police at Roebourne — the area indicated on the photo's caption — after he was released from imprisonment on Rottnest Island. Maybe it's old Bobby Roberts; we can't be sure.

What impressed me was how Aunty Hazel claimed and 'owned' him; it's typical of her to confront, rather than avoid, unpleasant facts. The shocking photograph provided an image of what she'd long grappled with: an ancestor with his own people in chains.

It's a problem for us: what to make of such an ancestor?

Usually, 'black trackers' were sent to work in countries far from home, but Bobby apparently chained up other Noongars. Arguably, many different groups made up those now known as Noongar. Maybe that's still the case, and perhaps after some generations of oppression we need time and space to reconcile amongst ourselves, even with those we might call brother and sister, before being rushed to reconcile ourselves to the status quo in other matters.

One thing's clear anyway: Bobby Roberts didn't divide people according to race, and he wasn't in the habit of thinking himself a victim.

Captain J Hassell, like George Cheyne and many of those jostling for land, complained of 'continual outrages committed by the natives.' Isolated and outnumbered, mistrustful yet needing a labour force — it's no surprise the colonisers sought alliances with significant individuals.

When a certain Noongar escaped from prison, Captain Hassell

chose not to inform the authorities of his return 'home' — to land occupied by Hassell — and concealed him from the police.

Why?

The man had 'influence,' said Hassell. 'Natives are quiet when he is here.'

Around 1850 the 'sub-Guardian of Aborigines' at Albany recommended that a certain Noongar be pardoned his crime because he was such a good influence on Aborigines of the Jerramungup district. Mr Trimmer thought the man, who he called Bobby, would make a very good policeman.

*

See, Hassells went looking around for Aboriginal people. Well, for land I s'pose it was. They made friends with people from Bremer Bay, and some of them were camped up at the Hunter River. That was Grandfather Bobby; he was there, old Grandfather Bobby Roberts. (His son Pirrup was also called Bob.) They made friends with him.

He used to communicate with the people down in Bremer 'cause there was whalers and sealers there then. They took him and his family and the rest of his tribe. When Grandfather Bobby went to Quaalup, he didn't have a wife, only his mother and father and that.

Quaalup was the first place Hassells settled out this way. They looked around for property and a good place for sheep and that and they found Quaalup, and of course it had the soaks and the spring on the hill, so they went and settled down there at Quaalup with their few sheep.

They were at Doubtful Island, 'cause there used to be a

freshwater swamp there, and Noongar shepherded sheep for them there.

Well, old Bobby took off over to Quaalup, and he went away on an expedition looking for property for Hassells. They travelled, him and old Hassell, they went everywhere, just out of Fraser Range and looked around there.

Well, when they came back they settled for Jerramungup. Bobby was only a young man then.

Bobby, he went with Eyre and Forrest and Roe, and they made him a good man. He done a stealing, but they forgave him. Hassells spoke well of him, after they pardoned him, after he been in trouble. He was like a boss-man, he kept the Noongars all intact, and kept law and order, you know.

They gave him the Blucher boots and the britches, they give him a hat and a gun, they give him a stockwhip.

They made him a police tracker.

I reckon that it's really sad, to think that those people in chains … They reckoned that those people was Bobby's own relations.

Daddy used to say that great-grandfather was a good man, and the white people liked him because he helped the white people a lot, but he said most Noongar people hated the sight of him, because he used to go and grab the people what did wrong. There used to be a lot of sheep stealing going on down in the Ravensthorpe area.

*

I couldn't find evidence to support Aunty Hazel's claim that Bobby Roberts also accompanied Eyre and Forrest, although the dates —

1849 to 1870 — are feasible. Roe, Eyre, Hassell, Forrest ... from Aunty Hazel's perspective I guess they're much the same.

She explains the relationship between Bobby and the Hassells in these terms: 'He done a stealing, but they forgave him ... they pardoned him ... he kept law and order.' A younger generation is inclined to read it differently. Is it stealing if your rights and home have been taken from you? Look at that photo again: it's hardly surprising that 'white people liked him, and most Noongar people hated the sight of him.'

I hadn't anticipated finding someone like Bobby Roberts in my family history.

Bobby Roberts wasn't the only Noongar accompanying the colonisers as they moved east in the latter part of the nineteenth century. At least one other of his countrymen also helped explorers, pastoralists and police. The archives mostly refer to this individual as Fred McGill, although once or twice he is named Tickenbut. Despite my discomfort with some of his decisions, I greatly admire him.

Twenty or so years after guiding the explorer John Forrest, Fred McGill went to the Esperance Chamber of Commerce and requested some land be set aside for Noongar people. He had no success. To help Noongars participate in the cash economy, he organised men to cut clothesline props and, after dancing for the townsfolk with his cousins, he chastised the audience for their stingy donations.

In the 1930s some of our people were still trying to raise money by dancing:

Natives Corroboree
Natives Yorkshire Bob and
Moses Wybung

Wish to notify their friends that a
Native Corroboree will be held on

Parade Street Reserve
At 7 p.m. to night

———————————

Work with natives, like our white
brethren, has been scarce, and we
much appreciate the kindness of the
'Albany Advertiser' in publishing
this brief note for us free of cost.

ROLL UP! ROLL UP!

And bring your spare coppers and
sixpences to help us.

Unlike Bobby Roberts, Fred McGill learned to read and write, and his letters to the Goldfields newspapers around the turn of the twentieth century show his sense of betrayal and injustice but, like Bobby, he apparently helped pastoralists 'disperse' other Indigenous people. One writer has suggested that some Noongars, having suffered a 'brutalising process … had formed the conclusion that there was no defeating the European invaders and that it would be best to take their side rather than continue sporadic resistance which was always met with blood retribution.'

Perhaps.

Fred McGill apparently helped the pastoralists against Ngadju — a neighbouring Indigenous group — but Bobby Roberts, Aunty Hazel said, fought against other Noongars.

I guess 'black troopers' had various motivations. Police work offered them an alternative to subsistence on the fringes of such a rapidly changing world, and while they were paid substantially less than their white counterparts, it was more than they got anywhere else. Some may have been fleeing tribal justice, or the sexual constraints and politics of traditional society. Away from town the tracker had power; the police were dependent on him, and he could take them anywhere he wanted, even lose the track altogether.

There may have been even more motivation for a Noongar to accept 'unofficial police duties'. Any power is attractive, and necessary, in times of rapid change. Bobby got a gun.

It's hard to know what to make of him.

He may just have been a brutal, opportunistic man.

He may have become so isolated and fearful that there was no alternative to co-operation, and so he admitted defeat, gave up.

Or Bobby Roberts, having come to know influential men in the new colony, appreciated their power, saw himself as their equal. I very much doubt he wanted to give everything away — his land, his rights — only to start at the bottom of colonial society and work his way up as if he were a convict, a stranger, or someone who had to prove himself.

Whatever the case, our Bobby Roberts appears to have gained an appreciation of innovation and strategic thinking, acquired political acumen and ruthlessness.

Very modern skills, really.

Bobby Roberts made alliances relatively early in colonial history. Confident and generous with people like Roe and Hassell, he also apparently learned how to look after his own interests.

And Fanny Winnery, my ancestor — what was her place in all of this?

Bobby Roberts must have been her father, Aunty Hazel said. The paperwork I'd found had her father's name as Wonyrin or Wongin, and another time as Winnery. Was that his Noongar name, then? The archives also told me that Bobby was among a group recruited to hunt down, among others, his nearly-namesake, Cape Riche Bobby.

Fanny Winnery

Our Grandfather Bobby, what went with Septimus Roe, he took Cape Riche Bobby's woman. Grandfather Bobby, him and another fella, they drowned that man at Cape Riche.

Cape Riche Bobby was a blind old man, an old man. His girl that they took was promised for him, *talak*. You know, the woman had to go and stay.

Bobby — old Granny Winnery's father — his missus he got from Cape Riche. He brought her from Cape Riche. Cape Riche, Pallinup, Hunter River, that was her area.

Old Grandfather Bobby, he had a brother but I don't know who that brother was called. He had a son, and the son was taken away to New Norcia mission. And there was another sister, but I don't know …

He had two wives.

Fanny Winnery must've been born in the Bremer region. Must've been up towards Hunter, 'cause that's where they all was camped, you know. I don't know who the other sister for Fanny was. I couldn't work it out. See, if white people wanted to keep records of you they kept them, you know, but they only said about the good ways they treated people, they never said about the bad way they treated them. They never said about the way they split the family up. They only printed all the things about Bobby, about when they give him a gun and made a big hero of him, you know. But as for Bobby's brother and Bobby's sisters ...

Bobby was the first Bob, and the next Bob was Pirrup, and Pirrup was the storyteller that told all the stories to Mrs Hassell. She's printed all the stories that Pirrup used to tell her.

Bob Roberts, Pirrup, he was brother for Granny Winnery.

They took her away when she was a little girl. She went away. That's how she got with them other Noongars. Well, Grandfather himself, he been down to Thomas River too.

Old Bobby had a sister, too. Her name was Julianna. This bloke came out of the water; I think it was down at Bremer Bay. He was a German bloke I think. His name was Dimer. He took her away, down Esperance way. Went with Campbell Taylor, Thomas River. Then stayed out that way. She was only about thirteen or fourteen.

Yeah, Dimer was a whaler, and he took Julianna, and he lived with her. They had another sister, but I dunno where she ended up.

Years ago they used to take 'em you know, they used to take the kids away. Always did that, if they could.

Fanny Winnery was with Mason, shepherding for Taylors. Taylors had farms all along there, before.

They went from Doubtful Island to Warriups, from

Doubtful Island to Kendenup. That was a run for the sheep, for the shepherds.

The whalers and sealers was before that.

Daddy told me that Grandfather Bob's old sister — Pirrup's sister — was Granny Winnery. He said she married a Coleman. They were migrant people, from South Australia.

And Cape Riche was Hassells, Hassells used to have a trading ship, Hassells and Moirs. Always pull into Cape Riche. They used to pull into Doubtful Island, to Bremer, from Bremer to the mouth of the river, from mouth of the river to Boat Harbour, from Boat Harbour to Swan Gully, and from Swan Gully to Cape Riche.

They used to cart, before the train started. They used to cart stuff to the outposts. And the teams, musta been camel teams, unna? Bring all the stuff to Balladonia, and they had a hut there. And then people looked after it. Left the stuff there, and then they took whatever they had, skins and that, to take back. These fellas went with the wagon train, brought from Balladonia to Esperance way, and from Esperance way they turn around and bring 'em this way to Ravensthorpe. Musta been like a shuttle train, unna?

She — Fanny — was with Hassells at Quaalup. Bobby was the one that took Hassells to Jerramungup and showed them the place there. He went with Septimus Roe and them to Fraser Range. Thomas River too.

They were all taking womans back in those days, and dumping them, and bringing another woman back.

Yeah, your family, the Colemans ... Your grandmother was, you know, your great-grandmother, she married a Coleman.

Old Fanny Winnery, she had two daughters, didn't she? She had two daughters. That's right! Married Coleman twins. And after that one of their girls married the Scott.

Yeah, Fanny's *daughter* married a Coleman. Aunty Ellie and them used to go down and see Granny in 1932 — 31 and 32.

They used to walk from Jacup to Needilup, and go. Sometimes they'd be away for four or five weeks. And when they came back, that's when those fellas give them a horse. They give them a horse.

Uncle Fred Rogers was down there, too.

When Uncle Booker and Mummy was down there, Daddy was breaking in horses for a Coleman.

Aunty Ellie and them used to go down there all the time, 1931, 32.

They wasn't just Ravensthorpe people; that was Esperance way to head of Bremer people. Winnery.

They must've been working down at the Hopetoun district too, because your father's photograph's in the hotel down there. Like he was only a little boy down there at Hopetoun.

The other Scott — your father's father's brother, old Oliver Scott — he went away with Aunty Margaret Griffin. Went to Kalgoorlie, I think.

We'll get it sorted out one day anyway, gotta work on it.

We're gunna take you and show you all the roads, we're gunna show you all the roads. And all the waterholes — *ngamar* — and things like that, you know. And go and show you the footprints and all there.

*

It took a long time to get to those footprints.

As grateful as I was for Aunty Hazel's acceptance, I was also impatient to 'get it sorted'. Once again I crosschecked oral history against the scanty written records.

My ancestor Fanny Winnery gave birth to a daughter at a place called Thomas River, east of Esperance, and the child's birth was registered several hundred kilometres away in Albany. On the birth certificate the father's name is given as John Mason, at other times he's called Jack. It was a name I remembered from a letter written by a member of the Dempster family, one of the early pastoral families on the south coast:

> ... other names I remember along the South Coast in those days, were Peter Henrickson, Harry Dimer, and Jack Mason. These were kangarooing and working where they could find work between Israelite Bay and Mary Ann Harbour — later I believe Hopetoun. They often used to call in at the cove ...
>
> (Dempster cited in Rintoul)

Dimer was another name Aunty Hazel connected to our Noongar people, and it's plausible that Bobby Roberts' sisters and daughter were companions and guides to these white men. Together they travelled that narrow strip of Noongar country bounded by the sea and by other Indigenous peoples with whom, today, many Noongars have family affiliations.

The archives agree that after Dimer had escaped his ship, Campbell Taylor hid him at the Thomas River lease. Mason, in between working as a seaman and teamster, also worked there. Taylor had interests in other properties along the south coast, and may have had Mason in mind when, in 1889, he wrote of shepherds who'd taken Noongar women as their companions:

Jack Tar's case is one which illustrates such a union. In the early days at the far-'off station where he was shepherding, the 'gaffer' took a trip to the nearest town, several hundred miles off. Jack was the boss in the 'gaffer's' absence. Shortly before this some natives were placed on an island for sheep stealing, and a young native girl was deprived of her promised husband by this administration of justice ...

As he was a very troublesome thief, it was likely that he would not be liberated for several years. In the meantime the young lady lived with her brother and his wife who, being good natives, were promoted to minding a small flock. At shearing time the youthful charms of the deserted fiancee so struck the manly Jack that a good deal of time was spent in the evening learning the native language after the day's work was done. The largest and brightest handkerchief from the store found its way to the damsel's head and shortly afterwards a dungaree gown with seams all sewed with palm and needle like a sail was presented to the young lady. After certain tribal negotiations had been entered into the fickle maid accepted the fortunes of her white lover and gave up all thoughts of her countryman on the island. The wedding ring of gold adorns her shining black hand now, and though her native man has long since been free she has never abandoned her honest Jack who has always been kind to her and her pretty children. She is an excellent shepherd and generally minds the sheep while her husband stays in a camp and cooks the food and washes and mends the clothes, or is busy making new garments for the children, all of which garments have the seams sewed in true sailor fashion with palm and needle ...

'Jack Tar' is an old British expression for a sailor. There can't have been many sailors working for Campbell Taylor who also married Aboriginal women. Dimer eventually did, but in different circumstances. Was 'Jack Tar' in fact Mason, and the girl Fanny Winnery?

A 'promised' woman would come such a distance, especially in such historical circumstances, and while Taylor may have confused her brother with her father, I'm sure he would have had no confusion about who was, or was not, 'a good native'.

The passage is something of an anomaly in Taylor's writings, as if he's struggling to keep the individuals contained within the roles he's allocated them. Despite the mocking, condescending tone, it's partly a story of cross-cultural romance and honour; the lowly white man learns his intended's language, recompenses the promised husband, and — in a remarkable reversal of gender roles — attends to domestic duties.

Taylor stumbles in the writing, can't quite position himself, can't find quite the right attitude. Is it a tale of romance and honour, or of a white man foolishly committing himself to one Aboriginal woman with trinkets, language and love? Does guilt tongue-tie Campbell Taylor and prevent him from revealing just how helpful 'good natives' are? Or is it the fact of a white man accepting — and being accepted into — Noongar ways? Then again the power and role of a black man with extensive networks and who'd already been this far east with John Septimus Roe decades ago might be what it's hard for him to put into words.

Taylor's equilibrium is threatened.

Fortunately for him, commonsense — sureties like Social Darwinism, and notions of social class and racial superiority — reassures and comforts him, and allows him to turn away from addressing the significance of certain individuals, and the value of other ways of thinking. He need not confront the extent to which he exploited those whose land he also stole.

We admire the two individuals at whom he sneers.

There are other paper records of Fanny Winnery and her immediate family.

In the 1930s the Chief Protector of Aborigines, A O Neville, began to inquire after Fanny's children, now adults. He particularly wanted to know whether her son — also called John Mason — was 'half-caste' or 'quarter-caste', because that affected how the law related to him. One of Neville's clerks summarised the Chief Protector's own enquiries in an adjacent area:

> Whilst inspecting the camp at Norseman on the 1st inst., the Commissioner questioned Dick Nine, who is quite an intelligent native, about John Mason.
>
> Dick stated that he knew John Mason who lived at Esperance. He said that John went to the War but he had not seen him since. Dick used to play with John in his young days but said that Mason was some five years or so his elder.
>
> Dick informed the Commissioner that he knew John Mason's mother. She was a full-blood named Fanny Winnery. He did not know anything of his father. He said that Fanny used to live at Esperance and Thomas River, and that he had seen Fanny several times. Dick reiterated that she was a full-blood and that she lived in a camp.
>
> Dick said that his sister, Minnie Jacobs, would know John Mason and his mother Fanny Winnery, and Sergeant Kevan undertook to question her next time she came in to Norseman. Dick was warned not to speak to Minnie about the matter.

Mr Neville harassed Sergeant Kevan, who eventually sent him a handwritten note:

> I have interviewed old Minnie Jacob re the parentage of John Mason and she informed me that a full blood native woman named Benyin was the mother, and a white man named Jack Mason was the father. Benyin died some years ago at Ravensthorpe and Jack Mason is also dead ...

Their marriage certificate calls her Fanny Pinyan, her father Wonyin. Her death certificate — rare to have such paperwork attached to a Noongar woman in 1913 — says Fanny Winnery, and names her father as Winnery. You can see the problem of trying to fit the sounds of one language to the alphabet of another. Both she and Mason died in Ravensthorpe, but their graves are not marked there, and the burial records name J Mason, but not the wife who shares his grave.

Aunty Hazel and her brother Lomas Roberts have shown me many an old grave. Sometimes it's a mound of stones in what's become a depression in the earth; sometimes there's even a cross. No mound of stones, no headstone or cross marks the grave of John Mason and Fanny Pinyan Winnery, that English man and Wilomin Noongar woman from the head of the Hunter River near Bremer Bay. She died in the house of her son-in-law, Daniel Coleman, one of twin sons of an Irish couple. Mr Coleman, the twins' father, apparently came to Australia as a convict.

Daniel signed Fanny Winnery's death certificate, identifying her as a 'domestic servant'.

Daniel Coleman was — for a time at least — in a business partnership with the Dunn family. A name, as Aunty Hazel informed me, with infamous associations for those of us descended from Western Australia's south-east coast.

Mist over Cocanarup

They reckoned John Dunn was killed because he had an argument with one of the old men. One of the old men speared him.

It was Granny Monkey's brother, Yandawalla, that killed Dunn, you know, for what he was doing to the women.

The truth was, Esmeralda Dabb was thirteen years old when Dunn raped her, and him and the overseer were busy satisfying themselves with the young girls and they locked all the old people up in the harness room.

And when she got away from them, she went down and got the men, see, all the young men there was having meetings there. They were shepherding sheep down the bottom, and they were having initiation ceremonies, you know. And she went and told the men, and when they come back they all, you know, they come back and they speared him, they killed him. Yandawalla speared him, at Cocanarup.

It's not very far, Cocanarup to Ravensthorpe, only about four miles. Actually, you can see Ravensthorpe from there, and look back and see the farmhouse. That's how close it is.

After John Dunn was killed, the other bloke, the overseer, got away. He got in touch with the Aboriginal Affairs department, or the government of those days, the government people; sent a morse code message on the telegraph line, and got a permit to kill the seventeen people that were residents of that place.

But then, they didn't say that there were Aboriginals visiting, come for a meeting. Nobody knew that other people come from Jerdacuttup and Hopetoun to be there. Initiations, you know, and to talk about marriage. You didn't have to come from Ravensthorpe, because it's quicker cutting across.

Jerdacuttup people got killed there, with the Ravensthorpe people. That's why there was so many. They were all one mob. It's only about twenty-five, thirty mile radius.

Old Dongup, he used to have a lot of connections with them. Old Henry Dongup, he used to travel and meet family, and he reckoned that altogether there was over thirty people that were killed down there. Thirty-seven people that he knew of were at the place at the time of the massacre.

But they covered it up, you know, the white people covered it up and they didn't want to tell other white people what went on, see.

After Mum and Dad got married in Carrolup, Dad took Mum down to Esperance to meet some of the family, and on the way he wanted to take her and show her where his mother's family were massacred.

So they went to Cocanarup, they travelled by horse and

cart from Borden. In the afternoon they got to a place called Jacup, and Cocanarup is not far from Jacup.

Dad wanted to show Mummy the massacre site, see. Where the family got slaughtered. She wanted to go there, and she was allowed to go there because she was accepted, and you're not allowed to go places unless you're accepted into the family, tribal way.

Just before they got to the actual site, Mummy said she wanted to go bush, you know. Go to the toilet.

She went behind a bush and while she was squatting, she noticed a singlet there. She thought it was a singlet. After she got up, she went and got a stick. She scraped the leaves away, see, where this thing was showing, and it all come to pieces.

It wasn't a singlet, it was like a tunic. You know, the old khaki clothes the troopers wore years ago, woolly ones. It was the buttons, the brass buttons. They picked up about eight or nine brass buttons, so the person that they killed there must've been wearing an old soldier's tunic or something.

They picked up the buttons, and Mum reckons all the cloth was frayed and it fell apart.

There were bones too. There was no legs, only the torso and the hip bones and that. The foot part and everything was all gone. The arms and head were gone. But there was these buttons laying around.

So what must have happened, must've been wild dogs. Wild dogs musta got at the body, 'cause there was a lot of dingoes in that area.

Mummy reckoned old boy went and got the bark and went and scraped all the pieces up together and went and put 'em in the overcoat and took 'em away. And he went away and buried them.

They would have been the first to go there for a long time, apart from old Dongup, and different old ones. There weren't many Noongars anyway, to go there. It was taboo.

We young women, like the girls, we were never allowed to go to the place but they used to go and visit — Aunty Ellie, Uncle Dongup, Uncle Abel, Grandfather Hughie and them, they used to go there, and others come from Ravensthorpe to go and have a look at the place.

They did take some of the bones, and they put 'em in the cave, Grandfather Dongup and the other old people that went there. But must've been the dogs got this one they missed, and Mummy reckoned Daddy wrapped them up and put them away, in the cave.

I don't know if you've ever been there — I've never been there — they reckon they've got this big mound, not far from the shed, and that's where they were all buried in a mass grave.

They reckoned they were all buried there in a mass grave, but I don't think they were, because people been finding, you know — even Aunty Ellie and Uncle Dongup, they used to go in there and just have a quick look and just go away again. They never used to stay, and they kept finding bits and pieces.

They're talking about heritage now; they're gunna list it, you know.

Would it be because it was one of the old places where white men first settled, or could it be it was the first place where the white man was, so-called, murdered? Or would it be because that's where black people's lives were all taken so senselessly?

So, white man's gunna have it now, more or less as a showpiece, the scene of a murder, of a massacre and that, and people will be going around looking at those places. It's morbid, unna? A lot of people, tourists, will go and look at the place.

A lot of people don't go there for the right reasons. Sad, really. A lot of people died there. We lost a whole group of people there. Why should a lot of people die for the one white man?

We're not allowed to go there. They got a fence and a sign on the gate saying, 'No trespassing. Keep out. Private property.' Last I heard, it belongs to the Boy Scouts now.

Lomas — Uncle Lomas — he went through the fence. Just like Aunty Ellie and Uncle Dongup and Uncle Abel and Grandfather Hughie; they used to always go through, go through and have a look.

And you know Kimmy, it seems a bit funny that different times when our people travel and been going down, some of them's cars have stopped and they have trouble, just like the spirits are trying to stop them, and telling them not to go past.

One of my cousins died in Esperance Hospital and we — me and Tex, you know Tex, my man — went down that way. When we got near this side of Ravensthorpe it would've been going on for ten o'clock and we were pushed for time, see, we were trying to get to Ravensthorpe clear-eyed.

Old boy driving along, and we went past the Fitzgerald, and the moment we got right to the river, we got to the Phillips River and crossed over the river, and to Cocanarup …

Well, you know, this mist came up to meet us, and you couldn't see the road. I say it was all misty, it was just like a big thick cloud of smoke, just like you were going through a bushfire, and it was just going in waves and then he put the wipers on and I was gunna say to him, let's stop for a while till it clears, and then I got to thinking. You know, it came back to me. I know the reason why. Must've been old people crying, see. I didn't say anything to him, because he don't believe in the things that we believe in.

I think that must be family crying, they probably know that I was going to see Malcolm and Malcolm was dying, see. Anyway, when we got to Cocanarup, where the road goes in, it just cleared like that. I wasn't frightened. I was more relieved, you know.

*

In the last few years of his life, one of Aunty Hazel's brothers — Uncle Cedric (Chubbo) Roberts — established a family corporation, the Weirlamun (Wilomin) Aboriginal Corporation, to protect the interests of the descendants of the Wilomin people, particularly those who lived in the Cape Riche–Bremer Bay–Fitzgerald River–Ravensthorpe region before colonisation. The corporation's constitution requires that each member must be recognised as a descendant of one of the traditional Aboriginal families of that region.

It stumbles along, this corporation. Aunty Hazel invited me to her grandson's house for the annual general meeting. Unfortunately, I arrived after the meeting was over and when most had left. In my absence Aunty Hazel had explained to everyone how I belonged, and talked about the work we had begun doing — this book, as well as some tasks related to it, such as the consolidation of 'cultural capital' within our community, and how to ensure its transmission and regeneration. I was only there for the eating and drinking, the smoking and yarning, the settling in the smoke around a backyard fire. Close in the darkness a voice said, 'Oh, what happened at Cocanarup means a lot to us.' It moved me, to hear it said and to think about what it implied.

What happened at Cocanarup around 1880 helps explain what that Noongar elder meant when, after I'd mentioned that my family had lived in Ravensthorpe, she said, 'I hope not, for your sake.' Obviously, she was referring to the killings, and perhaps also to the consequences for any Aboriginal people remaining there. I've suggested the insistently recurring phrases 'the first white man born' and 'the last full blood Aborigine' characterise an attitude to history and identity, but I now wondered about those who, like my ancestors, didn't neatly fit into either of those categories. Is there a way to maintain connection with an Indigenous heritage, a sense of kin with ancestors, while living in a world overwhelmingly hostile to such ideas? And how would you speak of such an event within one family whose different members might identify with either perpetrators or victims?

In contemporary public discussion we seem to prefer to distract ourselves from consideration of such massacres by arguing about numbers, quibbling over semantics. Exactly how many died? Was it a battle, or a massacre? Did it really happen? Where's the proof?

It's scarcely entitled to be called discussion when, biting and snapping, speakers retreat and turn away from such an uncomfortable topic and the emotional energy it arouses.

I haven't yet seen any definitive first-hand documentation of the Cocanarup massacre, that reprisal killing. There's plenty of references to it though.

'In the early days ... there was a lot of tribes there. The Moirs shot some and the Dunns did too ... they got permission to shoot the natives too,' said one 'pioneer', Gordon Cavanagh.

Another non-Aboriginal person, Marion Brockway, writes, 'Terrible stories abound, but cannot be verified, of the vengeance exacted by John's brothers on the Nyungars. One story is that a number of Aborigines were killed and buried in a mass grave near John's grave, the site being marked by a circle of posts. The rest of the Nyungars in the vicinity were chased eastward, the Dunns poisoning the waterholes on the way back, to prevent them returning.'

In his family history, Cleve Hassell mentions that the three remaining Dunn brothers 'declared war' and took it in turns to go shooting Noongars while one was left at home with their sister. He writes that a great many natives were shot.

H E (Spike) Daniels, a policeman who lived in Ravensthorpe as a boy in the early twentieth century, said:

> An Officer of Police was sent out from Albany to oversee what was called in those days an 'open season'. I believe that men, woman and children were killed. One group was chased for miles towards Lake Dundas and no-one returned. It is also said that men and boys were killed and women and girls left … When I was a boy in Ravensthorpe on a school picnic, we found the skeleton of one of the murdered Blacks. The teacher hushed it up and put the bones in a box and kept them. There is no doubt that the bones dated from the massacre … It is true that since the massacre, Nyungars have avoided the area although this avoidance may have been exaggerated by some …

My father told me that his mother — my grandmother — went to school with Spike Daniels. I wonder how she felt when the teacher put a finger to her lips, turned away with the boxful of bones.

Although I never met my grandmother, I remember visiting her brother in Hopetoun when I was very young and we had first moved back to the south coast. We called him Uncle Will, but others called him Bill. Years later I found a record of his understanding of what happened at Cocanarup, although curiously mediated by the writer, Laurel Lamperd:

> Mr Bill Coleman ... heard it by word of mouth from some of the participants of both sides who took part in the incident, though the incident itself happened a hundred years ago ... The writer has no evidence that John Dunn had sexual relationships with aboriginal women but it is acknowledged today that many white men, especially men living without white women did. If John Dunn did have such relationships, he would have been obliged to follow Aboriginal law. Whether John Dunn knew about this law or the penalty for breaking it, is a matter for conjecture, but it is doubtful whether the Dunns would have known much of the aboriginal language or culture.
>
> John Dunn was working at the station with one of his workmen when the aboriginal execution squad of four arrived. The aborigines enticed John away into the bush where he was held down and the execution carried out.
>
> If this had been an aboriginal 'uprising', John Dunn, together with his workman and any other men on the station, would have been killed on the spot.
>
> The family of an aboriginal so executed would have accepted the punishment but John's brothers, Walter, Robert and James, were naturally indignant about their brother's death. After the unsuccessful police search for John Dunn's executors, the three brothers were given permission by the authorities to shoot fifty aborigines, be they men, women or children, in retaliation for their brother's death.

*The Dunns loaded packhorses with supplies, returning
to the station to load fresh supplies when these were
exhausted. Aboriginal watering-holes were the first areas
where they searched. The remains of a human skull could
be seen in the early part of the century at the Undarrupi
watering-hole which is just over a kilometre north of the
spongolite quarry on Moir's Road.*

*When the killing began, the aborigines fled, and the
Ravensthorpe area became a taboo country.*

My grandmother's brother had it by 'word of mouth from some of
the participants of both sides.'

Is that a privilege?

Accounts by other elders have been published about the
Cocanarup massacre, and refer to the 'depopulation' of country
between Gnowangerup and Esperance. I used a quote from such
research (submitted to the 1984 Seaman Inquiry) as the epigraph to
my novel, *Benang*:

> *Many Nyungars today speak with deep feeling about this
> wild, windswept country. They tell stories about the old folk
> they lost in the massacre … The whole region has bad
> associations and an unwelcoming aura for them. It is a
> place for ghosts, not for living people.*

I'd like to think my father, grandmother and great-grandmother
were maintaining a presence, but it must have been hard, living there
and then between Cocanarup and Jerdacuttup. Perhaps they were
like ghosts; mere traces of what they once were, might have been.

I wonder: how did the man I knew as Uncle Will get to hear the
story from 'both sides'?

Making alliances

Aunty's Hazel's brother, Lomas Roberts, invited me along on a trip he was making to show an anthropologist some 'significant sites' as part of the preparation of a Native Title case. We'd be based in Ravensthorpe, and while we were there he wanted to look up a Mrs Cox and ask her about some Noongar families whose connections to Ravensthorpe he disputed. Mrs Cox was a white woman, he told me, who knew a lot about the history of Ravensthorpe and Hopetoun. Her family had lived there for generations and Uncle Lomas had first met her when she came up and introduced herself to some of the family sitting on the grass at Hopetoun and told them she had a lot of photographs and stuff she'd like to share with them. Uncle Lomas thought it was lovely of her to come up to us like that.

Every chance he got, Uncle Lomas tried to get in touch with Mrs Cox, and as we drove Ravensthorpe's few streets I noted that Dunn Street intersected with Scott Street. There were no streets called Mason or Coleman, and although you could find those names in the Ravensthorpe museum the name Winnery was nowhere to be seen.

Eventually we succeeded in finding Mrs Cox at home and, reminiscing, she and Uncle Lomas revisited names and events and previous discussions. Gerald and Josh Williams were with us too, and they reminded Mrs Cox that she'd rented her house to their sister. There was a lot to talk about. Mrs Cox went through the names of Noongar people she'd known over the years. 'And you must have known Kimmy's father,' Uncle Lomas said.

'Oh yes,' she said, bursting into a smile. 'I went to school with Tommy Scott.'

She remembered my grandmother too. I listened closely. I heard that she was a lovely, gentle woman. 'Kathleen'd sweep the yard every day,' Mrs Cox said. 'It was mostly sand.'

Sweep the yard? Sweep sand?

'Yes, I used to wonder about that. None of *us* ever did. But, that's what they used to do in camp, isn't it?' Mrs Cox said. 'So they could see tracks if anyone or anything came in.'

Aunty Hazel said you used a *barang* bush to do that, but I guess a broom did the same job.

'Pa Coleman,' Mrs Cox said, referring to Uncle Will. 'Pa Coleman was a wonderful man.'

She told us his mother — old Mrs Coleman, Harriette — kept a vegetable garden and how she'd walk out of town with a rifle on her shoulder and carry back the kangaroo she'd shot. Somehow, she had a house for all the girls, and a house for all the boys. The older ones were like adults, they helped look after the little ones.

I wondered what had happened to all my grandmother's siblings. I'd met two or three. There must've been cousins staying there also.

'But really,' Mrs Cox continued, 'we never used to think of them as … well, they were just people, you know. We were all just people.'

I wonder what parts of the bush Harriette Coleman visited and who went with her, who she met on her hunting trips. She must have had a network of support in the Ravensthorpe community. There would've been good people, and Ravensthorpe wasn't — certainly not after Cocanarup — a town overly threatened by a Noongar presence.

There's a photograph of Fanny Winnery's daughter, Harriette Coleman, when she was a young wife. She has quite fine features, perhaps the genetic inheritance of those Mrs Hassell describes in *My Dusky Friends*:

> *Our tribe was a fine looking race. They had beautifully shaped small feet and hands, exquisite filbert-shaped nails, with the half-moons well showing. Some of them were of a decided Jewish type of countenance, which I never could understand, for they were away from any chance of a Malay strain, being between Bremer Bay and Esperance Bay, on the south-east coast of Western Australia.*

In the photograph her face is very pale, perhaps heavily powdered. The hand around the baby on her lap is dark. Her husband stands beside her, one hand on her shoulder.

I found the image in the archives with lines slashed across it to indicate the donor had reclaimed the original.

Was the donor ashamed of those hands, that colour?

The photo's handwritten caption said, in part, 'first boy born in Ravensthorpe.' The phrase has a familiar ring, but is not quite the same as 'first *white* boy born'. It would've been impossible for the Colemans to make such a race-based claim without being challenged, but they could still insist on being part of a new community.

I don't know which of their descendants or in-laws donated and then withdrew the photograph, but I'd like to think the people in it were proud of a heritage which preceded the new community, and of being among the firstborn in a new society with its roots in the old. But perhaps there wasn't the language to express such a concept. Perhaps there still isn't. And perhaps, unlike Aunty Hazel and me, they had no such idea in mind at all.

I have another photograph of Harriette Coleman when she's a much older woman, sitting at the centre of three children. The two

Harriette Coleman, centre. No date.

youngest are on her lap, and another stands at her side. Harriette Coleman holds them all within her embrace, and the child at her side has her arm across her old granny's shoulders. When I was writing *Benang* I kept this photograph on my wall next to the photo captioned *'Three generations reading from right to left'* from that old book that asks its readers to consider the place of Aboriginality within the wider community. Each is a snapshot of generations, and I suppose each could be seen as a congratulatory 'trophy' photograph about Aboriginality diminishing, disappearing.

Except that the second photograph shows a collective embrace, hands holding onto one another. It's not people in a line; it's people gathered together and being inclusive. I'd like to think it suggests another way of thinking than the first. Aunty Hazel told me that tears came to Uncle Lomas's eyes when he saw this photograph. Because he recognised the family likeness in the old woman, and thought of our reconnection — or because he saw the younger, fairest children distracted by something outside the frame, and thought of skin colour and people fleeing from their Noongar family? It could be for either reason, or for both at once.

Aunty Hazel remembers the old people visiting Pirrup's sister, 'Granny Winnery' in the 1930s, but Fanny Winnery died in 1913. John Mason, her husband, was already dead, and at the time of her death she was living in the house of her son-in-law, Daniel Coleman.

He himself was dead by the 1930s, his brother and wife had, I think, moved to South Australia, and Harriette Coleman was the oldest member of the family remaining in Ravensthorpe.

Was Aunty Hazel wrong? Or did 'Granny Winnery' also refer to Harriette?

Harriette Coleman's father was a white man — John Mason — not Bobby Roberts. So why would she be known by the name Winnery, and as Pirrup's sister?

Was it because Bobby Roberts and Jack/John Mason shared the one woman, Fanny Winnery, and thus Pirrup and Harriette were what western genealogy would call 'half' brother and sister? Or perhaps Pirrup and Harriette were, in western parlance, cousins, because Fanny Winnery was in fact old Bobby's sister? If so, Noongars might well call Pirrup and Harriette brother and sister. Or was brother and sister a description of a different sort of close relationship within the framework of such things as moieties and kinship with a particular heritage and region, rather than immediate genealogy?

Then again, perhaps the name Winnery was retained because it signified a particular place, and the people who belonged there.

I asked Aunty Hazel about Harriette and Fanny: which one was Granny Winnery?

'Well,' she said. 'I don't know really, I suppose. Must've been Harriette then. It's that name, see, Winnery. I don't know, not for sure. We can't. I only know what people said, like Aunty Ellie and old Dongup. And what Daddy said, that your father was our people. Cousin, he said. I believed him, and I still believe 'em now. They knew what they were talking about. They kept track of people.'

I didn't like it. Suddenly, ours seemed a tenuous connection, and there were no papers to help me out.

'That's white man's stuff,' Aunty Hazel said, as if my reliance on paper was a disrespectful challenge.

Her emphasis was on the authority of the old people's word, and their sense of the importance of place. I respected that authority; I liked that belief in the significance of being descended from a specific and Indigenous tradition, of being part of a community of descendants, and I wondered at the possibility of something more meaningful than a simple biological kinship.

But I also like genealogical diagrams and sheets of paper. It bothered me that, shuffling my notes and diagrams, I couldn't be sure whether Aunty Hazel was of my father's or my grandmother's generation. Should I even be calling her Aunty? She shrugged her shoulders and said, 'maam-yok.' It meant, she told me, 'father's sister' and when I hesitated, she suggested another word the old people used, 'kayang', which, she said, translates as 'old woman', but respectfully, as in 'female elder'. I'd never heard the word before, but found it in a word-list provided by Paddy Coyne, a past elder of another Noongar family associated with the south coast, where its meaning was given as 'aunty'. Others translate it as 'grandmother'.

Okay. It was the language of our place. It said the right thing in both languages, and was as straight and sincere a word as I could find.

It was frustrating for Kayang Hazel, I think, how slowly I put this book together. She must've got a little impatient, especially once most of the taping and transcribing had been done. I agonised over the editing and how I might complement her words. It wasn't easy to tease out details, weigh nuances, consider the tensions and contradictions — partly because she's very deaf, but also because she wasn't interested in such things. Once or twice she said something like, 'We better leave that bit out. Might split up some of the family if we say it that way.' But mostly she let me know she'd had her say, the rest was up to me.

Still, I couldn't help constantly retracing the history we'd pieced together, trying to work out how our genealogical lineages connected and deviated. Despite Kayang Hazel's reassurances, the realisation of the discrepancy between the old people visiting 'Granny Winnery' in the 1930s and Fanny Winnery's death in 1913 made me worry at it all the more.

Kayang Hazel began her genealogy with Bobby Roberts. She repeated what she'd been told, waved a provocative photograph of people in chains.

I had papers leading me back to J Mason and Fanny Winnery. A white man and a Noongar woman who may have become his partner in ways respectful of Noongar law, or may have been 'stolen'. It's probable that some male colonists partnered Noongar women with the consent of elders, and it's clear that some were killed when they behaved like disrespectful barbarians. Noongar witnesses at the trial of one of the Noongars accused of killing Moir (in 1877, at Fanny Cove) said he was killed because of the women. Dunn (in 1880, at Cocanarup) was killed for similar reasons. Mason and Winnery's first child — Harriette Mason — was several months old when her birth was registered only a few days after Moir was killed. It would've only taken those few days to sail from Fanny Cove to Albany, and old man Mason knew a lot of the people who sailed to and fro along the south coast.

Another of their children — a boy named after his father — was registered within days of the 1881 acquittal of one of the Noongars accused of killing Dunn at Cocanarup. Perhaps that acquittal, as much as a simple desire for revenge, motivated the prolonged reprisal killings suggested by some of the accounts, even though white men with their own ideas of justice had already punished most of the killer's people.

By contrast, John Mason, in the context of this continuing clash of black and white law — or, since there was that one acquittal, the continuing clash of black and white peoples, the latter at least with an apparent pragmatic disregard of their own law — registered his children's births. Not only is it possible he obtained Fanny Winnery's family's consent to make her his partner, he also married her, in Albany in 1884 — the same year Dimer escaped his ship and spent time with Bobby Roberts' sister at Campbell Taylor's remote Thomas River lease.

John Mason might have thought official paperwork would provide a degree of protection from the revenge of those fixated on race and intent upon 'depopulation', and would validate the partnership he'd made. On the other hand, claiming his wife and children through 'white' law may have been a way of consciously separating them from their surviving extended Noongar family, and thus been an element of the very apparatus of conquest.

I prefer to see John Mason as a commendable man, even if the birth and wedding certificates only ever refer to his female companion as 'Fanny — an aboriginal'. After all, perhaps it was the officials, rather than John Mason, who weren't interested in her Noongar name, thought it unimportant. I wanted to find something like love, something like equity in their relationship, even if Mason, like Dunn and Moir and many others, was initially just another white man who grabbed women and took them away. 'Always did that, if they could,' said Kayang Hazel.

So maybe J Mason was a good man, lusting and loving; maybe he was a villain. And Bobby Roberts? I'd prefer all my ancestors to be heroes, but Kayang Hazel seems less sentimental than me in that way.

*

Grandfather Bobby? Great-grandfather? Everybody — Noongars — didn't like him because of when all them people got killed at Cocanarup — the white people was the ones what killed 'em, you know, but Old Bobby mixed with them, and they were the people that murdered Granny's family. Old Bobby knew the Dunns.

While he was going around chasing these people that were doing silly things — sheep stealing and stealing from settlers' huts and that — old Bobby went to the Wilomin people. Wilomin people top end of Quaalup. There was a colony of

Noongars there. That's where his son, Grandfather Bob (Pirrup), got his first wife, Monkey. She belonged to the Wilomin tribe.

Like, our grandfather had two wives. He had our grandmother first, and her name was Monkey. Her name was Ngoorir someone reckoned, but everybody says Monkey. Terrible really, but we all say it Kim, we all use the name the white man gave her.

She was born in Ravensthorpe, and that was all her family what them fellas got. It was Monkey's brother, Yandawalla, that killed Dunn, you know, for what he was doing to the women.

Pirrup's other wife, Emily Dabb — Karribi was her name they reckon — was born in Hopetoun. That's where the Dabb family come from, from the Jerdacuttup region, that's their region. Hopetoun region. And most of that family got killed there, too. Some of them got killed, but there was some of them down at the river too, see. They stayed away.

Daddy reckoned that his old father, Pirrup, used to tell him, and his grandfather told him, that there was only about eleven of them left that lived mostly down in the Fitzgerald, between Ravensthorpe and Bremer.

Our grandfather, he went and took Monkey away, took old Granny Monkey away. And Granny Monkey was promised to one of those people from that tribe. They used to travel up and down, come from Hopetoun way. And Granny Monkey was from down Ravensthorpe, travelled to Hopetoun.

But she wouldn't go with them when they went to get her. They were supposed to take her halfway and then meet him. She went away and lived with this old wadjela man, and Grandfather went and grabbed her, and belted the old wadjela bloke up. He flogged him up. And he brought Monkey away with him. Monkey, that's my dad's old mother.

They came back to Jerramungup. These other fellas told 'em they didn't want 'em there. Because they thinking there's gunna be trouble with these other fellas what coming from the hills side, you know.

He took her with him to Kendenup. Hassells had property there. Well, some of these people that were down at Kendenup must've had some connection with those people, 'cause they all got hold of old Grandfather and they flogged him up, and they belted Monkey up. They said that they were married wrong way, he went wrong way with her. So Hassells picked him up and they took him to the stations.

*

Kayang Hazel says Bobby Roberts worked with the police and the pastoralists, even those who kept and mistreated Noongar women. She says he stole a woman from Cape Riche Bobby.

Kayang Hazel's grandfather Pirrup's first wife was the sister of Yandawalla, who had killed Dunn at Cocanarup. Pirrup's second wife was known by the Christian names Martha and Emily, as well as Mudda. For the sake of convenience we keep to Emily in this record; she always had the name Dabb, and was one of those who escaped the Cocanarup massacre. Kayang Hazel reckons Bobby Roberts chained up some of the Dabbs.

I had to wonder: did Pirrup take the two women — 'Monkey' and Emily Dabb — as part of the spoils of conflict, as a reward for the alliance he and his father made with the white men?

And yes, perhaps Bobby Roberts introduced his sister to Dimer, and similarly arranged a woman for Mason. Is that how my two ancestors got together? Did Bobby Roberts arrange partners for white men, sometimes in accordance with traditional authority, other times in defiance of it? It might've been that way; I don't know. If it was, it may have been sexist of him, but it certainly wasn't racist.

Assisting the pastoralists as they moved eastwards from Albany, establishing their leases, Bobby Roberts must've been middle-aged. He'd been that far before at least once, when he travelled with J S Roe in the late 1840s. There'd been continuing decades of trouble and conflict and Noongars were increasingly being sentenced to Rottnest Island Prison and — unofficially — to some of the islands off the south coast.

I think it's likely some south-coast Noongars did initially marry non-Aboriginal allies and friends into their own family and that some, if not most, of those allies then flouted the customs and laws into which they'd been accepted. Alliances were formed and alliances were broken, often violently.

I'm emphasising the welcome Noongars initially provided, and their inclusiveness, but it's on the record that Noongars also repelled and resisted. Hassell, for instance, was obliged to recruit individuals to help mollify Noongar hostility. There are numerous references to spears being brandished and to bushfires as a form of attack. Sometimes hundreds of sheep were driven away at a time, a tactic which would've deprived the colonists of their major food source.

Sometimes Noongars who had initially been quite welcoming later became the resistors. Fred McGill, for example, railed against injustice, and used the colonists' means to do so, protesting to local authorities and writing letters to the newspapers.

But he and his people were outnumbered. Resistance was called 'theft', or 'absconding'. Resistance was breaking white law. Resistance was trying to avoid conquest, was adapting different strategies to maintain certain values even as others fell away. Resistance was merely surviving, and in such circumstances there must have been a lot of slippage, a lot of compromise and shifting ground. Even now, merely considering such reduced possibilities, it's hard to keep your feet, let alone stand tall.

Mason and Winnery were certainly mobile, living at various places along the coast between Albany and east of Esperance. Occasionally they even travelled as far inland as Norseman and Balladonia. There are many lovely camping spots along the south coast, and one — a little to the east of Hopetoun, between Jerdacuttup and Fanny Cove — is now known as Mason's Bay.

We don't know its Noongar name.

Winnery and Mason's children learned to read and write. I've found no records of them at a school or mission, and assume their father must have taught them. In 1897, when she married Daniel Coleman, the Australian-born son of Irish parents, Harriette signed her own marriage certificate. Her sister Dinah married the twin brother Patrick who'd helped his brother bring the Clydesdale horses and loaded wagon across the Nullarbor from South Australia. The wedding certificates give their 'usual place of residence' as Point Malcolm, a grassy, well-watered place where teamsters camped to unload the boats and carry supplies to the inland goldfields. Mason's signature is prominent on the marriage documents.

At the cusp of the twentieth century, almost twenty years after Dunn was killed at Cocanarup, the policeman stationed at the soon-to-be-proclaimed town of Ravensthorpe notes that John Mason and his sons-in-law are camped nearby. There is no mention of the women.

Mason is granted some land around Ravensthorpe, but loses it after neglecting to 'make improvements'.

The Coleman twins fare better; they're hard-working business people and tradesmen; teamsters, miners, blacksmiths, fettlers. They've got tools and the technology to utilise the strength of their powerful horses. They're also members of the Australian Natives Association, a patriotic organisation dedicated, among other things, to Aboriginal welfare. Of course, their wives weren't members of the Australian Natives Association. Being women, they weren't eligible and, being Aboriginal, they weren't entitled to citizenship. Nevertheless, the Coleman men claim and care for their Noongar wives and children — no easy task in a tiny frontier town. Perhaps, as 'native Australians', their sense of national identity allowed some inclusion of their wives and children's Indigenous heritage, but even so, that inclusion must've had definite limits.

Good, decent men, I'm sure, looking after their own.

Despite the 'depopulation' of the region, there were a few people in Ravensthorpe other than my immediate family who better fitted the stereotypical perception of what it was to be Aboriginal. Ravensthorpe police books over the years mention some of them. The Dunn family have an elderly individual living on their property into the twentieth century. Now and then individuals receive blankets or rations. A few — other than these Colemans — seem able to move in both white and black communities. Someone is betting at the races, another features at a sports day; someone is exceptional with horses, another marries a white man.

In 1916 and 1917 two Noongar men requested exemption from the Aborigines Act, and even though the police supported their applications they were refused. Unlike the bureaucracy, the police in Ravensthorpe must've been flexible and tolerant of those they knew had proved able to move in white society.

The police must've noticed when Henry Dongup and Ellie Roberts came visiting my ancestor, Harriette Coleman — who Ellie Roberts called Granny Winnery when she talked to her niece, Hazel Brown. Very likely, they were regarded as intruders.

The 1932 police report mentions only two children living with Harriette Coleman: a son and a nephew. Her daughter, my grandmother, would've been about fourteen. I don't know where she or her other brothers and sisters were. I don't know what happened to the 'separate accommodation for boys and girls' that Mrs Cox had mentioned. Mrs Coleman is described as a widow, and as 'having married a white man' in 1897. All three individuals are classified according to their caste; that is, divided along racial lines.

The police accept Mrs Coleman's help in doing the necessary calculations, and in telling them she is 'quarter-caste' she manages to escape the legislation of the time. A few years later — or even a few years earlier, and with a different policeman — she might not have been so fortunate. Kayang Hazel clucked her contempt for such words of evasion when I told her about this, but it's a way of thinking, a way of dividing people that even Bobby Roberts must have come to realise. Sure, it wasn't his style; it was the way of the pastoralists and police.

Even though Granny Winnery had developed a network of support in the town of Ravensthorpe by the time Henry Dongup and Ellie Roberts came to visit her, the police report of that visit initiated a series of letters between the Commissioner of Native Affairs and various, apparently reluctant, police officers. The commissioner had to remind them he was waiting for a reply, and so a policeman wrote:

> (the) younger generation of Colemans are mostly grown up and some are married and have families. Of the younger generation some are at Ravensthorpe, while others are at Broomehill, Collie, and South Australia.

When she died in the 1940s, my grandmother was living in Perth, the capital city of Western Australia. She was with a Scotsman, whose brother also partnered a Noongar woman descended from a local family. Many of these individuals — including my father's and grandmother's generations — lived among the white community.

Today, descendants of J Mason and F Winnery are spread further and wider than country towns of the south-west, some in the 'black' community, some in the 'white'. Some move in both — which may effectively be the same as being in neither.

A cousin of my father's rang me after reading one of my novels. I'd never met her. An elderly woman, she told me of waking up as a child and screaming at the sight of 'this old black woman' leaning over her. It was the first time she'd met her grandmother, the woman known to some by the Noongar name Winnery, to others by the name Coleman. She said she had nightmares for weeks afterwards. Skin colour and legislation had moved her away from country, from language, from her Indigenous heritage.

She'd learned, among other things, a certain way of looking at people.

Once, when she was a child playing with other children, a truck pulled up and men jumped out and started shepherding all the children onto it. Then one of the adults called out, 'No, not that one, that's Will's daughter,' and they separated her from the others.

Her father was the man who'd heard the story of Cocanarup from both sides, and seen the evidence of a skull.

As an adult she once — once was enough — parked her car in a south-coast town to breastfeed her baby. Someone spat on her, called her a 'black bitch' and told her to get out of town.

Kayang Hazel named a Noongar man who was six months old at the time of the Cocanarup massacre, and was raised by a white family in the district. In a letter, Uncle Will refers to him as a friend. One of that man's grandsons told me the old man could speak Noongar fluently, but if you closed your eyes and listened to him speaking English, you'd think it was a white person speaking, someone really well educated.

The man has since passed away, but one of his daughters, herself now an elder, says her father told her he came from South Australia.

I guess you might say something like that, if you were a survivor of a massacre, living among a community founded upon the massacre site. It'd be very hard to tell your children the truth, and at the same time offer them a future. Perhaps it'd be easier to say you came from somewhere else, that you were something else again than 'the other'.

An enthusiastic Hopetoun historian contacted me after he'd read my novel, *Benang*. He'd known Uncle Will — Harriette Coleman's son — and spoke of him as a sort of 'renaissance man'; a fine mechanic who also built his own house in Hopetoun, liked to paint in watercolours and acrylics, and was a great source of knowledge about the region. He told me about Ravensthorpe Museum, and when I got there I read about Uncle Will delivering a lecture to the CWA explaining the meaning of Noongar place names like Jerdacuttup.

There was also a letter from one of Uncle Will's cousins, Ethel Standley, written in 2000. She was born at Ravensthorpe in 1905 and lived there until 1926. I'd never met her. The letter is addressed to a Ravensthorpe heritage committee and expresses disappointment and anger that her and Will's fathers are not acknowledged among Ravensthorpe's pioneers:

> Looking back over a lifetime of experiences and living I've
> drawn my own conclusion as to why my family have been

*ignored. Racism is as strong today as it ever was, and, as all
the earliest settlers knew ... my grandmother was ...
Aboriginal — hence our ostracism. Times have not changed
a great deal, but I feel very strongly about this ...*

In another piece of writing she acknowledges that she knows
nothing of the family connections of Fanny Winnery, her grandmother.
And is silent on the contribution of Fanny and her daughters.

Sad, I thought.

I paraphrased a small piece of Uncle Will's writing in *Benang*, a
novel I had almost completed before having these long, one-sided
conversations with Kayang Hazel:

*Can you understand, dear people, why I'm rather diffident
about discussing the early history of Ravensthorpe as I knew
it as a boy? The descendants have given their forebears
images which they wish to see and present to the public in
their most favourable light. It would be a continual source of
acrimony were I to join in their discussions. So I think it much
better for me to write all my thoughts down for the perusal
and study of my younger relatives.*

Well, this younger relative is grateful. I wish he'd written more.
And I'm grateful, too, that Kayang Hazel shared her memories and
included me as she has.

Only a few years before Fanny Winnery's daughters married the
Coleman twins, A Y Hassell rescued old Bobby Roberts' son Pirrup
from being beaten by other Noongars. According to Hassell, the
beating was punishment for Pirrup and Monkey for marrying the
'wrong way'. Hassell took the two of them back to his station.

A Y Hassell was J Hassell's son, and although the relationship between the Hassell and Roberts families has been preserved, it's certainly not the same as it was, and surely not the way Bobby Roberts intended it.

It's not like when Bobby, just back from his journey and conversations with surveyor-general Roe, showed J Hassell the best grazing land.

The Hassells recorded some of their perceptions of the relationship between themselves and Noongar people. *My Dusky Friends* documents aspects of life at Jerramungup station in the late nineteenth century, and Kayang Hazel and the family are sincerely grateful that the trouble was taken to write and publish it. Its author, Ethel Hassell, having arrived at the property as a young bride, describes her new house as 'like a fort'. She claims to have a friendly relationship with the Noongar population, but is furious the one time her 'dusky friends' stray from the woodheap and enter her house. She also mentions Pirrup:

> *My dusky friends were a great resource. Indeed, I often wonder how I would have got on without them, their unfailing humour and child-like ways, and merry laughs at such trivial things always cheered me up, never mind how low spirited I felt, and it was always with a feeling of pleasure I heard the cheerful, 'Missus have wongie (talk) today,' and we would adjourn to the woodheap and discuss every subject under the sun. I remember on one occasion one of the boys had told a deliberate lie and misled my husband about some sheep, causing considerable trouble. I thought to improve the occasion on one wood chopping day, got out my Bible and read the story of Ananias and Saphira, laying great stress on how they were struck dead in consequence of telling a lie. The boys went off as I hoped, duly impressed, but old Buckerup*

*who had joined the party (for being a mulga he did not have
to work or hunt, the tribe kept and fed him in return for his
services) lingered behind and remarked with a broad grin,
'That very good story, Missus, Pirrup make great bother when
he not tell um true, good thing to frighten him, but you and I,
Missus, know better, it only good for children.'*

I wonder what else Buckerup might have said? His dismissal of the
Bible story suggests he believed the Hassells weren't always so
particular about the truth.

Hassell undermined the authority of the older Noongar men
when he prevented them from punishing Pirrup and Monkey, and
made it unlikely they'd offer support to Pirrup another time. Pirrup
was thus isolated, and made more reliant on Hassell.

A year or so later, when Pirrup tried to move on from life with
the Hassells, he was arrested. His crime? Absconding from service at
Jerramungup.

Within a single generation an unequal partnership had been
confirmed as a master/servant relationship.

Bobby. Bob. A lot of Noongars on the south coast were given the
name. I wonder if it was a pun on the British vernacular for 'police'
and, if so, what each 'Bobby' gained by his alliance with the coloniser.
I reckon our Bobby Roberts would've felt the same as his
countryman, Candyup Bobby, who Campbell Taylor wrote about in
his local newspaper, the *Australian Advertiser*, on 30 July 1888:

> … *one of the few remnants of the healthy strong natives who
> inhabited this district forty years ago — an old man who
> takes his name from an estate near Albany where he was
> born … will gravely tell you that the white man who owns*

Candyup has no right to it, that it was left to him by his father long before a white man ever came on it, and here follows a long line of black ancestry truly quite an effort of any white man to remember. It is a curious fact that every native man has his own piece of ground, and as the tribes do not seem to have increased beyond certain limited number, no confusion has arisen. An old native will tell you the several owners of the land you pass over in a day's ride in the bush.

Taylor's article was published seven or eight years after the Cocanarup killings began, while several leases were still being 'established' along the south coast. Taylor's family had already secured property — Candyup, close to Albany, another at Oldfield River, and their newest lease at Thomas River, several hundred kilometres to the east. Candyup Bobby's predicament and protests show that the situation had changed remarkably in the relatively few years since Cocanarup, let alone the forty years since Bobby Roberts first helped out Roe and Hassell.

The pastoralists had gained security and confidence but — unfortunately for Noongar people — they weren't as open to partnerships and alliances as some Noongars had been.

Candyup Bobby, like other 'owners of the land you pass over in a day's ride in the bush' no longer had free access to that land. In those sort of circumstances you do speak 'gravely', argue justice and law, cite genealogies and other evidence of occupation.

Similar discussion occurs today, in Native Title forums for instance, and is often just as futile.

Kayang Hazel said Bobby Roberts and J Hassell were partners.

Bobby Roberts made strategic alliances. He paid his dues to the colonial society, and showed himself to be at least as ruthless, talented and adaptable as its recognised members. He'd travelled widely and had good networks; he knew the lie of the land and how to get things done. He'd learned a lot, and must have had expectations.

We don't know how or when his life ended, or even where his grave is. In the genealogical charts which trace families that were on the south coast in the nineteenth century there's an empty space around Bobby Roberts where you'd hope to see brothers and sisters, mother and father. Even Kayang Hazel struggles here. Perhaps his isolation led him to make the partnerships he did. It's similar with his son Bob Roberts — Pirrup.

Whatever the case, Kayang Hazel and I want to emphasise the fact that Bobby Roberts began by guiding, introducing and familiarising strangers with his land and its ways. He made certain dubious alliances with the colonisers, and may appear self-interested compared to others who shared his culture, but you'd think he and his children, all things being equal, were more than able to hold their own.

So however misguided Bobby Roberts may have been, what happened to his children and to subsequent generations was a betrayal of the partnerships he made with the immigrants, because within decades he and his family had become unwelcome strangers in their own land, and subject to the racism of the growing colony.

Soon after the beginning of the twentieth century, the infamous 1905 Act and its amendments institutionalised the disempowerment of Noongar people. It isolated them, and created a fault line between Noongars and wadjelas. Many of my most immediate family were stranded on one side; the wrong side, a lot of my friends would tell you. Isolated from their heritage and extended Noongar family, they were also, arguably, implicated in the process of assimilation. They were stranded one side of a divide, while Kayang Hazel's immediate ancestors were stranded the other side.

There's a fault line, a chasm, which separates Noongar from

wadjela, especially after the apartheid-like society that Western Australia was for at least the first half of the twentieth century.

If it was hard for Ellie and Dongup to meet with Granny Winnery in the 1930s, it was nevertheless a happy thing. But the distance separating them and their children grew larger, and became harder to cross.

It's still quite a journey.

Too kanya — too ashamed

Kayang Hazel wanted to tell me her understanding of our Noongar heritage, and about our Noongar people. It was experience I'd largely not shared, and she seemed to think that her family history was a way to explain at least some of it. She gave examples of the physical and psychological isolation of individuals like her grandfather Pirrup, who was sent all the way to Rottnest Island, a particularly stark and concrete example. I thought also of Fanny Winnery; of people like her and a different sort of isolation. I never got to tape Kayang talking about Pirrup's imprisonment, and anyway he returned. Not everyone was so fortunate.

One of Dad's brothers, Uncle Booker, was about sixteen or eighteen years of age when him and Pincher went to this shed and they stole. Pincher was old Grandfather's half-brother, his other name was Larry Williams. They had their own horses, but they stole a bridle, and they stole tents, and they stole blankets out of the storeroom. They went down to Cape Riche to meet up with the other tribes down there, gone looking for girlfriends.

When the Hassells heard they stole the tent, they brung the police on them. Police caught 'em asleep in the tent, see. They went to jail. Sent away to Rottnest.

You know, Uncle Booker never ever came back to Ongerup, not to Needilup, never went back to Jerramungup, never went back to Ravensthorpe, never went back to Esperance.

Uncle Booker did his time in jail, and when he come out he was frightened to go back, 'cause Grandfather brought him up properly, and they would have give him a good belting. Spear him, maybe smash him over the head. He was too shamed of himself when he came out.

Well, Hassells already had a station down there at Kendenup, and some of the family used to fetch his sheep from Doubtful Island and drive them down to Kendenup for the station. Follow the hills right around you know, drive the sheep. So, he stayed over there for a while and went to Katanning, then Kojonup, then Cranbrook.

Noongars were allowed to take up blocks of land down that way, so Booker got a block of land down there at a place called Shamrock and he stayed away. Built himself a little mud house down there, and it's still standing now.

Then he came back to us when we were in Borden 1952, or 51, and Daddy wanted to take him out to Jerramungup, to go and apologise to old Pop Hassell. But he was frightened, he was too ashamed, he wouldn't come.

He worked with old Claude Weller, who passed away now.

Old Claude Weller, Uncle Booker worked with him.

He eventually came back to Borden and Daddy said to him, 'Well now you here,' he said, 'we'll wait for Sam Woods to come, we'll go out to Jerramungup, I'll take you back to see old Ednie,' he said. 'You go and apologise,' he said 'for what you did when you was a young man. You go back and you say you're sorry.'

Uncle Booker, he reckoned no way, he didn't want to go back. Even though we took him down to Dillon Bay, this side of Bremer, he wouldn't go into Bremer. He didn't want to run into any of them fellas from Jerramungup. He didn't want to see any Hassells 'cause he reckoned he was too *kanya*, too shamed for what he did, you know.

And different times when we was out there living in the bush, and Daddy was doing anything around the district there, we'd go home for rations, go back to Jerramungup, go back to the station, go back and get the flour, tea and sugar, and old Pop Hassell would always ask for Booker.

'When you gunna bring Booker back to see me?'

Booker didn't want to see him; he didn't want to see him. Too ashamed for what he did, you know. Hassells had a lot of Noongars down there staying but they didn't really belong to the district, like that was more or less the ration outpost for Noongar people, you know.

Same as down at Ravensthorpe; Noongars travelling that way'd go to the police station to get flour and sugar.

Hassells at Jerramungup was like the outpost, and at Wellstead's when you was in that district round there you could always go for flour tea and sugar 'cause governments gave 'em like surplus.

Every time when we went back there, they'd get cartridges for Daddy, and we'd get the money for skins. We could always go there and get food.

Even old Jock Hassell used to ask for Booker.

Booker didn't want to have anything to do with them. He stayed away sixty-four years. Too ashamed of himself, see. His father, Pirrup, was a very respected man with the Hassells, and his father, Bobby, too. He worked with the Hassells.

This Booker disgraced them, you know. Him and Larry. Grandfather Pirrup told him he wasn't wanted there any more, he wasn't allowed to set foot in the place.

Daddy offered after all those years, go back and apologise.

'No way, they put me back in jail.' He couldn't see that, you know. Daddy said, 'No, you've done your time …'

'No,' he said. 'Kanya. I can't go back there.' But old fella — Ednie Hassell — he wouldn't have had a grudge against him.

And even Grandfather Pincher, Grandfather Pirrup's older brother, when he came out of Rottnest, he didn't come back. Well he went away with the Winmars, see. Old Winmar did his jail too. Pincher and old Winmar they went to Quairading afterwards.

He went to Quairading; he worked at York for a while then he went to Quairading. Stayed with the Winmar family. He had a block of land, got a block of land. He used to go round the district and break horses in for farmers.

They got a monument, put a monument for Pincher in Quairading town.

I didn't know. They were telling me, I went there for a funeral to Quairading. I went with my grandsons, Budji and

Danny, and when we got to Quairading I didn't want to go to church. I wanted to see my good old mate, you know, old Lindy Lou Garlett, Granny Garlett …

Danny said, 'While they're having the church service do you want to go out to Badjaling and have a look at the old mission?' Danny's old grandfather, old Kickett, that's where they was reared up, at a place called Darling.

We got out to Badjaling — they built these houses there, Winnie McHenry got one of them. I was that pleased you know, to be there. I went for a walk, at the old reserve. I seen these ashes and the moss over the top and I got a stick and I said, 'Oh somebody used to camp here.' And I stood on one side, see, and I felt like a feeling came over me, just like I been at that place before.

In Quairading, well everybody liked him and that. Someone said, 'White people thought a lot of Pincher, he was a well-thought-of Noongar.' As a matter of fact they got a plaque there now, down there at Quairading, with his name on it. So he musta been a good person, you know, but never ever, never went back to Jerramungup.

Oh, he could've come back; Daddy said he could've come back, but he was shamed, he did wrong, and he didn't want to be in the district. He was sort of kanya-kanya, you know?

Everybody liked him, he got on well with the Noongars up there in Quairading.

It was funny, you know, Kimmy, because … Well, not funny, it was real, and it was true. All the Noongars that was sent to Rottnest, you know, the majority of 'em, they never came back.

You get that book … they reckon it tells you the Noongars

that was there ... it tells you the ones that died there too. It was lucky for those old men that they made a break, and that they got away, eh? Otherwise they might've been killed over there.

*

One of the 'old men' who 'made a break' and escaped Rottnest Island was Jack Mindum. He leapt from the boat he'd rowed back to the mainland, grabbed a horse and rode the hundreds of kilometres home to the south coast. The other two men who escaped were recaptured.

I've seen the caves and groves where old Mindum hid in the 1890s, and the gunshots still echo in the archives.

After a time the police must have given up on him. Most Noongars learned to stay well away from the police, and Jack Mindum had more reason than most. He and his family lived and worked with the Roberts family. He was another man Kayang Hazel called grandfather. When he died on a farm at Needilup in the late 1930s, a horse and cart carried him to Ongerup where Pa Tjinjel and old Fred Wynne dug a grave beside the river and buried him. The policeman in charge of Gnowangerup police station observed, and a few of the dead man's extended family — Kayang Hazel among them — wept as the body was laid to rest.

Kayang Hazel said he went into the earth wrapped in a check shawl that Pa Tjinjel won at the 1937 York Sports sprinting competition in the short space of time between riding his bike from Jerramungup and bicycling home again.

Kayang Hazel says that Pincher and Booker were ashamed, but it seems to me equally likely that they resented the Hassells, and were bitter at being powerless in their own country.

In the early and middle 1800s many Noongars on the south coast of Western Australia had guided and worked with the immigrants. Of course, there was also conflict, and in the mid-to-late 1800s there's evidence that increasing numbers, wanting respect for their own ways and realising the injustice of the situation, resisted the demands of the immigrant society and were consequently arrested, imprisoned and banished from their country. Some died on Rottnest. The southern pastoralists also used other islands along the south coast as unofficial prisons. Some who survived such banishment never returned home. Others — like Mindum — hid away, furtively eking out an existence, dependent upon those who'd usurped them. By the mid-1900s, according to Kayang Hazel, 'they had the fear in them.'

These descendants of that tiny minority — no more than five per cent, say some experts — who survived the initial decades of colonisation had very little access to what had been their people's home for countless generations, and equally limited participation in the colonial society. Some Noongars were allowed a role as rural labourers — at first paid with rations, and later with not very much more, and always dependent upon the goodwill of the immigrants. A very few individuals — like Fanny Winnery and her children found themselves 'among the white people' and moved into the colonial society. Many others were evacuated from their traditional homes and interned with other Aboriginal peoples in reserves, missions and 'settlements' designed — so the rhetoric went — to provide vocational training. Children — generations of them — were especially targeted.

Growing up around Needilup

The first children taken to the Carrolup Native Settlement from around Ongerup were Clem and Anna Miller, Lily and Fred Wynne, Fred Roberts. Would've been about 1914. They took 'em from Toompup; got Bonnie Jean Woods too. Their great-aunt was looking after them. Most of their mothers had died.

Fred Roberts and Fred Wynne ran away from the settlement in 1916. People there got terrible treatment, and the black trackers who did all the bossing of the inmates were really brutal. They used and abused most of the young girls, and the real fair girls nearly all took husbands just to get away. Sometimes the girls ran away, but they tracked 'em down and brought 'em back.

The old people lived in camps on the other side of the river, and the young boys and girls were locked up in dormitories every night. People weren't fed properly, and the young people had to work, but pay or money was never heard of. They buried people wrapped up in chaff bags, and a lot of them died when they shouldn't have, because they didn't get medical treatment. Nearly all the babies were born in the camps.

The dead bodies were kept in the jail, a big mud and stone building with only one window with a thick wooden door and a big bolt and padlock. If you didn't do what they ordered, they locked you up in there, with the bodies.

My mother Nellie came with Maggie Williams, Daisy and May Dean. They were all taken from their mothers up in the Murchison area. My mother often told me how the girls were treated in Carrolup. She was unhappy and always afraid. They didn't always understand the ways and laws of Aboriginal people down here. Another five cousins joined them a few weeks later, and that was better. Better for her, anyway.

My mother was brought down from Carnarvon on a cattle boat. They kept them down in the bottom of the vessel and didn't let 'em come up top. It was a rough trip and they all got sick. From Fremantle they took 'em to Balladonia Mission, and then a few weeks later took 'em all the way to Carrolup. The white people musta thought they were gunna try to run away back to where they come from.

My mother did run away, but they caught her and made her marry my father, Fred Yiller Roberts. He had quite fair skin, they reckon. She was fifteen years old.

She died in 1975. She never ever saw her mother again. Most of the children sent down from the north married, and not many of them ever went back to their own people.

Different times now, they say.

When they were little, my kiddies were asked if they wanted to go there for the holidays. You know, Community Welfare ran a holiday place down there for children. But even though they've changed the name to Marribank …

Well, for the years they ran the Carrolup Settlement … well, just the name, it sickens you. They've changed the name, but none of us ever forgot that it was Carrolup. To us that was a concentration camp. And that was somewhere we had a fear of, and didn't ever want to be sent.

I remember Lionel Howard, who had been taken away from his own relations and didn't know why as he hadn't done anything bad. He came back to Borden, only to be caught again by the police and taken back to Carrolup.

He used to tell us many years later of the treatment he received there, and of the food they were given to eat, and how they were locked up in the night and flogged by the black police whenever they spoke up for their rights. He had a special hatred for these black police, and I remember one time telling us he was glad they were all dead.

Lionel was able to run away from Carrolup again and never ever let the police catch him after that. He was always very timid and frightened of the police and Native Affairs people.

Well, there was a lot of people like that … There was a lotta reasons to be frightened, for us to be careful, you know, back when I was young.

Like at the beginning, things were really good at Hassell's, but then when some of the young boys started to grow up they used to start to get into mischief.

I was always told that while we were living in the bush Hassells used to flog the boys and that, and were very hard on them, and very hard on the teenagers, but they weren't hard on all the old people. Everybody had to work for a living, and they gave them rations and that, things like flour tea and sugar. They always saw that they had medicines and that they were looked after, but ... see, how we were treated in the early settlement days, you might see 'em, our people, running around down there fetching white people a cuppa water and things like that.

Like a couple of those old men down there at Gnowangerup, old Henry Dongup and old Grandfather Moses, they never ever called a boss by their name. It was always Mister or Master. The women were always Missus. That's 'cause they had the fear from the old days.

Years ago the boss never called the kids by their name. They called all the boys 'Jacky'. They called 'em all 'jacky-jackies'.

Old Ednie Hassell was always interested in the family and what was going on. We could always go back, if Dad wasn't working, we could always go back and there was flour, tea and sugar there, you know?

And different farms that we were at, Ednie used to always check on us, once a fortnight; sometimes he'd come there weekly or once a month, and if we needed food and we'd run short he'd help us out.

We'd always go there for rations. They sort of helped us.

There's lots of graves in the bush because people, you know when they got dissatisfied with Hassell, they were all moved away, most of them all moved away from the station, and they were shifted and went back bush.

We moved around the Borden, Ongerup, Gnowangerup and Needilup area until I was about four years of age. Then we came back to Gnowangerup to live, about 1930. That's when

Fred Tjinjel Roberts, Gnowangerup, 1924.
(Photo courtesy of the South Australian Museum)

Fred Tjinjel Roberts (Pa Tjinjel) with wife Sybil
(Nellie Limestone), Ongerup, c. 1974–75.
(Photo courtesy of Ryan Brown)

Freddy Yiller died. My mother then had two children, so Fred Tjinjel Roberts — really the only father I've known — he married my mother.

They got legally married about two weeks after Fred Yiller Roberts died because that was Noongar way, you know. She was accepted Noongar way, and his brother died, and so he had to look after her. He had to care for her, and for us. And then about ten months after, my brother Stanley was born. We were living on a reserve, oh about half a mile from the township. Brother and Sister Wright had a mission house about two mile away.

On this reserve where we were living we had an old tin hut that served as a church and a school. And they had a hospital. It wouldn't have been half as big as this room, and I can remember it well, it had an open fire. My mother used to act as a midwife, and look after the women when they had babies.

If you lived in Gnowangerup you got what they called the government rations. The government gave the missionaries flour, tea and sugar, and tobacco, to share out among Aboriginal people, see.

We stayed in Gnowangerup for a while, and then Daddy said, 'Well, not worth staying here, we might as well go somewhere else to raise the kids and give them a better life.'

Daddy took us out to Needilup. Dad used to go around the district shearing in the season, but we stayed at Charlie Brown's farm, and Dad worked all through that district.

This is a few years after my own father died, and Dad's old sister, Aunty Ellie and Grandfather Dongup, they came over to stay with us. That was the years when they used to go to

Ravensthorpe to see Granny Winnery. There weren't very many other Noongar people in that area, just my father's cousins and their relations. His younger brother Malcolm was married to Connie Williams. They used to come out Christmas time.

Uncle Malcolm and Aunty Connie worked for Mr King and stayed on Mr King's farm, about four miles away from Mr Brown's. And Daddy's other cousin Sandy Mindum, he stayed not far from us, maybe about five miles away. We used to see them on weekends. Apart from being at Brown's, Daddy used to shear at Carney's. We used to go out to Peacock's, and Stark's, all the farms around that district.

We stayed at Brown's until 1934. We were quite happy there. We had an old shack made of bag and tin, a couple of tents and a great big shed. We made our own fun those days. There was Mummy, Daddy, myself and Stanley. And Lenny. That was the first children, and in 1932 one of Dad's step-sisters came to live with us, Margaret Williams. Her mother died, in Gnowangerup. Her old father brought her out.

Daddy used to go out and set snares for kangaroo, 'cause you could sell the skins, you know. You used to get about one pound ten (they used to call it thirty shillings then) for one good skin.

He used to skin the joeys too, and peg 'em. Mummy used to scrape the skins and tan 'em and cut 'em into squares. She used to make blankets. Well, they ran out of cotton thread one day. We used to buy it in big reels.

'Ah well,' I said, 'can't do any more sewing.' We used to sit down and watch Mummy sew and sew. She used to make blankets and sell them to farmers and travellers, you know. That sort of helped us keep going.

But there came this time when the thread ran out.

So she used the sinew from a roo tail. They cut the tip of the tail off, and they pull it, and when the tail comes out this sinew comes out. You pull it all into pieces, make it like cotton, and dry it. Sometimes before you dry it, they twist it on a bone. When it's dried it's just like thread anyway. And Mummy used to use that to sew the blanket.

She had one big needle like a darning needle. And Aunty Ellie said, 'You know you can make that needle.'

'How?'

They used to have oilstones, rasps, axes, three-cornered files.

'Well,' Aunty Ellie said, 'I'll show you how.'

Mummy didn't know how to do this, Daddy didn't bother to show her, and neither did anyone else. She didn't have to do it before she met my father.

In a kangaroo's arm, there's that long, skinny bone. Anyway, Aunty Ellie got one. She filed it right down, filed it right down. Made it real skinny. Then with the corner of the file, she made a hole in it, for the thread to go through.

She made Mummy two, three of them.

You could do that out of hard wood too. Aunty Ellie used to do that out of sandalwood. Make a needle, make the point, and then burn a hole through the head part. Then you pull the thread through. She used to do it with sinews, too. She used to make us boots out of the kangaroo tail, and moccasins, you know.

She'd sit down and scrape the skins. Nothing was ever wasted. Used to sit down and take the sinews out of the tail, and use the boomer skins and that to make the carrying bags.

Noongars were very efficient, only because they were taught by their people. It was more or less about survival.

Daddy was working on the farm, but mostly he made money trapping dingoes, doing skins. In the weekends he used to trap dingos. But this was during the depression, 1930 to 1933, and he worked for Charlie Brown for five bob a week.

When Stanley grew up enough and Margaret came to live with us, we girls were able to take care of him. Then Mummy started to take over snaring kangaroos, pegging skins. We made the pegs. You dry the skins, roll 'em up, take 'em into town, send 'em on the mail truck. Send 'em away and the money comes back.

It was a good life, you know. The boss let you kill sheep, at Brown's farm at Needilup.

And in 1935, Mum was pregnant and we went back to Gnowangerup. And she had my brother Aubrey.

After Aubrey was born our family consisted of four kids, and we went back to Brown's. We had relations all round, we used to see them at Christmas time. Browns were terribly good white people, because Daddy had been working with the two Brown brothers ever since they came back from the war. We stayed at the Browns until 1936.

In 1937 we went back to Gnowangerup. I used to go to school with the white children; Aunty Mag and Lenny and myself went to school. Audrey was born then.

The Aboriginal people had shifted from living on the reserve near town, most of them. There was a block of land about three miles from Gnowangerup, and Sister Wright made a mission there. And Audrey was one of the first babies to be born up there. I think she was the third baby to be born at that particular place. Well, we stayed there then and Daddy used to go to Borden and shear all around. Around 1938 we stayed in the mission and went to school. We stayed and my mum had treatment for her bad eyes.

We'd been at the mission before, right at the very beginning of it, for a few weeks. This was even before the people started to build the mission house. We planted a lot of trees which are still there today.

My mother knew Sister Wright when she was back at Carrolup, and she wrote her a letter and told her there was a lot of Aboriginal people in the district, and how the ones she had made friends with had asked her to let this good Christian white woman know that they all would welcome her and wanted her to come and help them as all of them wanted to live as free people.

*

Sybil Roberts, who came to Carrolup with the name Nellie Limestone, must've been quite a woman. A photograph taken at Limestone Station before she was sent to Carrolup shows her sitting with a white family. She's turned to look at one of the babies who's either crying or laughing. She's attentive, caring, and it's a cosy, domestic scene, even if her role — as the sole Aboriginal person in the group — was only as maid or nurse.

Apparently, her father was a white man, and we can only wonder why she was moved away from the family in the photograph in her early teenage years. She must've been doubly uprooted: taken from her mother and then, having adjusted to living within a white family, shipped out of the Murchison to the horror of Carrolup.

She must've felt vulnerable, married at fifteen years of age in strange country, still familiarising herself with the ways of Noongars who were themselves under threat.

Merle Bignell in *The Fruit of the Country* — her history of Gnowangerup — says that Gnowangerup Reserve was formed after Aborigines got in touch with Sister Malcolm, who they'd known at Carrolup. Kayang Hazel said her mother wrote her a letter, and as a result Sister Malcolm — who'd meantime married Brother Wright — came to Gnowangerup. Sybil Roberts assisted them, and was there again when the Wrights and Noongars moved from the reserve to the mission.

Other than living at Gnowangerup, the Roberts family alternated between farms and the bush. The need to educate their children must've made Gnowangerup compelling, especially because United Aborigines Missions — unlike many Aboriginal settlements — apparently tried to be inclusive of their population's lifestyle. They didn't separate children from their parents and they tried to provide rudimentary services Noongars couldn't access in town: a school, a shop, a church and hospital.

Brother and Sister Wright got complaints and harassment from groups like the Gnowangerup Agricultural Society, the Roads Board, and the local Department of Health. They stood up to them, and also the police, and people like the Chief Protector of Aborigines, A O Neville, and his representatives.

Noongars were disadvantaged, disempowered, and under great pressure. Sybil Roberts had become part of that Noongar community, affirmed by her marrying twice into a family that maintained links to its traditional country, extended family and elders. Even as wife, mother and midwife she was a pragmatic activist more able than most to move between the white and black communities.

The shire council's recognition of her at the opening of a

community centre for Noongars in the 1960s (reproduced in Bignell 1977) does its best to diminish her contribution:

> At the opening the shire council presented Mrs Sybil Roberts with an easy chair in recognition of the example she had set in the past to other reserve residents (Mrs Roberts had been one of Sister Wright's small charges at the Carrolup Settlement).

Hazel Brown, seated, with daughter Valda on her lap, c. 1953. Right: Sybil Roberts. Left: family friend, Daphne. (Photo courtesy of Elaine Miniter)

Kayang Hazel has a high opinion of Brother and Sister Wright. I got the feeling that both mother and daughter appreciated the Wrights' efforts, and that, since Sister Wright had come to Gnowangerup in response to the call from Sybil Roberts, their relationship was not as simple and one-sided as the shire council would have us believe.

*

Brother and Sister Wright lived in Gnowangerup for all these years, and saw many of our people born and grow up and die. There was over two hundred people at the mission, everybody was happy, and the children went to school and Sunday School. The men worked all around the district; the ones who didn't find work picked wool and sold it to buy food and clothes for their families. I went to the mission school with my two brothers. Most of the girls and teenage boys went to work as soon as they left school. Those days you had to work hard and the pay was always poor.

Lots of times the boss from Carrolup — Mr Bisky, he drove a brown Ford car — would come and want to take away some fair children or perhaps a widow or someone who done something wrong.

Brother never wanted them to take kids and that. As soon as anyone used to come down in that car, Brother Wright always knew. They couldn't come on the mission because that was owned by the church, and they had to have Brother Wright's consent to come there and look around. They wanted women that had no husbands, or children that had no mothers, or the fair ones.

But Brother always knew that he was coming. Sometimes he'd come to the school and make an excuse. Maybe he'd say, 'Teacher's not well today' — we only had but one teacher — 'so you can all have the day off' — and he'd go down to the camp, all around on his old pushbike and say, 'Now I want all the big ones to take all the little ones away, and you boys to act as watch' — you know, lookouts — 'take 'em into the scrub.'

Or better still we used to take them into the paddock. And we stayed in the big scrub there, and there was a dam there. And then the mothers'd cook up food and the big boys'd bring it.

The big boys'd stay around, play football or pretend that they were doing something but always keep an eye on that car and where that man was and when he was on his way. And Brother'd go with him as far as town, come back, get on his pushbike and go out to the boys and say, 'Well, he's gone, youse can all come home now.'

All the time, we had that fear. Sometimes, when we used to see the police come in a horse and cart, come up in a sulky, we used to all go and hide, thinking oh well, if you weren't working they'd get you. I used to work sometimes in town, with Mum, before I went to the Richardsons. My mother used to wash all over the district. Down there with the MacDonalds for a while.

If they found a girl was not working, the police would come, take the girl away. That man in charge of that settlement, he always found excuses, you know?

Even if, say, someone used to run away with someone else's wife and they'd go and tell the police. Well, that was a criminal offence. They'd take you away to the settlement for six months or something.

Brother Wright had some Christian friends who had a timber mill down near Manjimup, a timber town called Wilga. This was where the timber was sent to from Gnowangerup mission and our men paid Brother whatever money they could afford for the timber, and also for the iron for the roofs. So cottages were built on the mission; one or two rooms, and much better than bag huts.

Aboriginal people were not allowed in Gnowangerup town after six o'clock. We weren't allowed to go to the pictures and the women all had to have their babies in the camp.

In about the early forties the government gave money for a two-ward maternity hospital, which was built on the mission and it was really nice. All the people were happy at the mission and Brother Wright ran a little store where the people could buy food and he protected the Aboriginal people all the time, always.

But the townspeople and other people made complaints, reckoned that Brother Wright was making profit from the Aboriginal people, and the mission got closed down.

All he was doing was buying the wool people plucked from dead sheep. He gave them a reasonable price for it.

Christian people used to send second-hand clothes to the mission but, well, not many people wanted to have charity. It sort of made you feel independent if you could pay something for things.

He'd maybe sell a good dress for about tuppence or thruppence or something like that. Well, when people had the money they bought things that they needed and I couldn't see that that was robbing anyone.

And while Brother and Sister were there, conditions on the mission were really good. You had proper medical attention.

Well, Dr Boyd used to willingly give that. And Sister used to get medicines, ointment, and eye drops and ear drops. But, those days, not many children had runny noses and bad ears, I can say that for a fact. Very few of them did.

Runny noses and that only came about when people started living in the houses with concrete floors. But Brother and Sister really helped, you know. The kiddies went to school regular. Brother Wright used to ride a bike around to every camp and you had to explain why you weren't at school.

Brother had a dam built there and that was clean water. The women carted water and washed at the dam. They washed their kiddies and they washed their clothes and everyone wore white sandshoes and socks to Sunday school. We only had the one-room church and that was crowded with people.

People loved to be looked after. Brother, he preached a lot, and he was a Christian, but we accepted that, a lot of people accepted that. The living conditions were really good. Some people used to have a garden. When they got their little shack, you know, they used to show pride in it, in their place, the little home that they had. But the government wanted them at Carrolup; that's why they said Brother was robbing the people.

Well, they were getting something for something at the mission. Because whatever they sold — the dead wool and that — they bought food. And they were sort of independent and even the men used to ride pushbikes to work. Brother used to fix up the old bikes and sell 'em, and when people were sick at Borden, Brother used to get in the old car and go and pick 'em up and bring them in. The only help people ever had was Brother and Sister.

After reports were made to the big bosses in the Native Welfare department that Brother Wright was robbing the Aboriginals in Gnowangerup, Brother and Sister were forced to leave. It seems to me they wanted Brother and Sister Wright out so they could close that mission down. Their place was taken by Mr and Mrs Street, who built dormitories. Then only the children of school age had to be looked after by the Streets and all the parents had to go back into the bush to live and find work where they could and fend for themselves.

Well, then they all drifted away, and Mr Street looked after the kiddies and that. And, well, they had no other place to come to, so Main Roads said they could shift back to Gnowangerup, to a place just up from the railway station. That was the old reserve, where Brother founded the first old mission.

Well, they went back there and they all camped around. Tents and bag huts and bush camps and such like. They had to go and leave the little homes that they'd built up at the mission, just to come back and live under the trees again. Well, there weren't any trees, just bushes. I guarantee there wasn't a tree at that reserve that was as high as a kitchen table. So really, they had no home, they were sort of shuffled to and fro. But all those years, they kept their tongues behind their teeth.

They didn't talk, most of 'em, because they were afraid to speak out. The police walked roughshod all over the top of 'em, and did what they wanted and not one said one word. One bloke said to me, 'Oh, it's all right for you, you live at Borden, you live in the bush.'

They said, 'You free out there. You haven't got a police station at Borden. We have police here every time anyone kicks up a fuss.'

*

The very infrastructure and authorities of white society caused the fear many Noongar people felt. As Kayang Hazel sees it, Brother and Sister Wright were removed because they were *too* supportive of Noongars.

Pa Tjinjel wanted to be somewhere else, to find 'somewhere to raise the kids and give them a better life,' but, in practice, the options beyond neglected reserves (designed to keep you out of the way but still available as cheap labour) were very limited. Sure, there were the poorly resourced missions, but despite the fact that many people have fond memories of such places, the very existence of reserves and missions within the structure of wider society suggested that you weren't wanted, that there was something about you that needed to be removed or fixed. It's the sort of experience that tends to breed shame, and a number of missions seem to have deliberately set out to do just that. But not Gnowangerup Mission, says Kayang Hazel, at least not when Brother and Sister Wright were there.

Many reserves and missions grouped people together as fellow survivors — because they were black — but otherwise they were often strangers who shared, if nothing else, the experience of racist oppression. Gnowangerup's Noongar population was made up of people who mostly knew one another. Such a combination — shared oppression and backgrounds — must've encouraged anger and a strong sense of collective identity. Perhaps despair and shame too, just from being the recipient of such treatment.

My immediate family line didn't have the experience of reserves or missions. I don't know that sort of anger, can't claim the same sense of a collective identity forged by the experience of oppression. I knew *something* about the shame — just from being 'of

Aboriginal descent' in the Australia I've known — and I knew something about the pride, if not how to adequately express and articulate it.

In part, this is why I followed Kayang's word so closely, and if there's a lot to do with racism and oppression in these pages, it's because it's so crucial to many of our Noongar people's sense of identity, history and justice.

I loved how Kayang Hazel spoke of the natural environment — the bush. Our ancestral home.

Again I listened closely, followed. I learned a lot, and came to understand — though perhaps I knew it intuitively — that the bush gave respite from the hostility of white society. It let you feel good about yourself, and it was that part of your country you might still call home. If it was being destroyed and remodelled to suit someone else's needs you had to try and go more deeply and secretively within it.

Kayang Hazel and her family spent time in reserves, missions, and the dwindling bush. They worked at the edge of wider society and the cash economy, mostly working for farmers.

Of course there were differences between individual farmers, just as there were differences between any individuals and between institutions and even between towns. Gnowangerup Mission was better than Carrolup; Borden was marginally easier than Gnowangerup. Although the wider society was apparently set up to disadvantage Noongars, white people varied in the extent to which they were unthinking and 'innocent' products of it. Not everyone thought of and acted towards Noongars in the same way.

Kayang Hazel describes the Browns, for instance, as 'terribly good people,' one of whom, cited in Galant and Wanless, had this to say about her immediate family:

... we always had aboriginals on the farm, when we were young fellows. They had a major effect on our lives because they sort of grew up as a family. The family that we had was a Roberts family. Dad employed Freddie Roberts for a number of years and it was during the years that we were growing up that his family was also growing up ... We learned a lot of their culture and got a good understanding of their way of life. I don't suppose their understanding of our way of life may not have done them as much good as our understanding of their way of life did, but unfortunately they seemed to probably glean more of the unfortunate aspects of our way of life ... Freddie Roberts was just a general farm hand. He was more-or-less employed for several years on a part-time basis, fencing and clearing ... there's still paddocks ... that are called 'Freddie's paddock' ... he cleared it.

Good people then, who recognised — albeit naively — that an unfair exchange had been made. The Browns and the Roberts — some of them at least — may well have been able to greet one another thinking 'people are people', but there's an obvious imbalance, a continuing bias favouring one group of people over the other. 'Freddie' Roberts (Pa Tjinjel), the third generation from Bobby Roberts, continues the tradition of contributing far more than he receives. I'm sure he had ideas of how things might be done, if not the opportunity to enact them, but instead, as an underling in his own home, he was obliged — forced — to make it less habitable for himself.

It must have been a bitter experience to fell the trees of your home country and have the raw earth named 'Freddie's paddock' as you're turned away with fewer and lesser places to go.

Kayang Hazel liked to talk about working on farms. In fact, she liked to talk about working in general, and about the ability to work hard as something worthwhile in itself, but I got the impression that she regarded an earlier time in her life as far more formative; a time when there was more freedom, even as she was learning to be wary of wadjelas and white society. Perhaps it's just nostalgia, perhaps it's something to do with looking back on one's childhood, perhaps it's because she had fewer siblings in those years and therefore got more attention and bore less responsibility but, despite the fact that they overlapped with the Depression era, she has fond memories of her early years. And strongest of all are her memories of when they were a family unit, and away from the towns.

Depression years

Sometimes we used to go away bush, put the horse in the cart. Daddy used to go and cut the beehive and get all the honey in the comb and bring it back and Mummy used to strain it all, put it in jars or tins.

Some days my Dad and Mum, along with Dad's younger brother Malcolm, who was married to Connie Williams, and the Mindum family, would all go out into the bush and find beehives and then the men would cut down the tree and rob the nest.

The women would strain the honey through a sugar bag and after that it was shared out between each family. This was what we had to sweeten our oatmeal and wheatmeal or whatever we needed to sweeten. It was sometimes used to sweeten our tea. If we had plenty Mum would make us lollies.

We'd go out when emus are fat in summer, shoot two or three and rend the fat down. Have enough fat to last you, then. Mummy used to make soap with fat and caustic soda.

Never wasted even the emu feathers; skin 'em and scrape 'em, or pluck 'em and put the feathers in chaff bags, hessian bags, flour bags. Make mattresses and pillows from them. It was hard work. We never had much, but we were happy.

I remember years ago, when we didn't have any flour and there was no shop there — the nearest shop used to be Ongerup and then the next Gnowangerup or then you had to go to Albany or Mt Barker. Aunty Riddlan got the mangart seeds off the trees, you know. You get all the dry seeds and then put 'em on a blanket and shake 'em all up, let the tips fly and that and shake 'em up and make it all clean and let the stuff blow away with the wind. Smash 'em up, grind 'em up. Get enough flour, and then make a damper, johnny cakes …

Lot of people, lot of Noongars, wouldn't have been fed like we were fed, and maybe a lot of them would've been too proud to eat what we had, but then we had to survive, didn't we? We lived out in the bush for weeks and weeks, and so we had to be able to eat what was there for us to gather.

Nothing was wasted.

Best part of my growing-up years was when Dad took the time off to take us hunting. Me and my brother Lenny, Dad used to teach us how to trap, track, hunt possums, how to find a goanna when it was sleeping in a hole, and how to set snares, how to hunt kangaroos. We were taught all about snakes. What snakes could kill you and where you were most likely to find dangerous snakes.

I learned to read from cowboy books. Mummy taught me to read. And we learned the essential things in life, you know, like respect, common sense. We knew how to feed ourselves.

We was taught to trap, to hunt, and things like snaring, and it would be nothing to go out in the bush for a full day and all we would take was water. We knew what to eat and how to get it.

When we lived out in the bush it was all scrub, because the white man didn't do very much clearing then. When we were travelling and we wanted water we could camp anywhere. Well, in the forties the land settlement took over and they started smashing down the scrub and everything has changed. When they did all the clearing down there, that's when they destroyed it, that's why there's so much salt now.

When the trees and that were growing it stopped the salt going into the water. Only one creek was salt water, all the others were fresh water. And gilgies, just packed in there. But now everything's all salt. Only place you'll find gilgies now is in the dam.

I was the champion person for possum, no-one could beat me for *koomal*. I could climb a tree just like that. Matter of fact, poor old Gerald Williams — Aunty Riddlan's boy — he nearly broke his neck one time when he was with me.

You know we went to Jerramungup once, and there was seven mallee hen nests between Jerramungup homestead and the cleared paddock over there; there was seven in that area.

One thing Daddy always taught us, if we found a mallee hen's nest — me and Lenny would have known just about every mallee hen's nest in the Jerramungup district, that's how mad we used to be for mallee hen eggs — Daddy always said you mustn't take all the eggs. Not like *karder* — racehorse goanna, you know — you can take every one. But *ngaw* — mallee hen — we always left one egg there for the mother. We never ever killed a mother mallee hen.

And if the egg had chickens in it you weren't allowed to touch them. You only were allowed to take the fresh eggs. You can always tell if a mallee hen egg is fresh. Because when they got chickens in of course they're heavy, and when they're freshly laid, they're light.

If you find a mallee hen near the nest you know that means there's fresh eggs there, because when she's finished laying she'll go away from that nest. They hatch themselves and they come out themselves. The mother never goes back to them. The father feeds them. The father eats the seeds and he comes back and vomits them up for the chicks. The father looks after the nest.

Same as a mother emu, she lays the eggs and it's father's job to sit on the nest and feed them. Mother's off and she's gone. She's done her job.

From our old people, we learned the rules. We were taught the rules, the traditions of Noongar people and the laws and rules of our old people. Everything was explained to us; we didn't have to go and read about it in someone else's book. What we knew, we learned it from our old people. You picked up language easily because all of our peoples spoke their own dialect, you know. We learned to speak our own lingo from when we very small.

We weren't ashamed, it wasn't kanya-kanya for us to talk Noongar way, it was something that came naturally, you know.

During that time there was a depression and it was dry, everything was brown! There was hardly anything that was green. The sun was hot, and it was dry, the only thing you saw green was a gum leaf, and the bull-rushes around the river and around the soaks and that.

We had to leave Brown's for a while and go to Carney's, because they had a soak down there. We went there and stayed for a while, and that was pitiful you know, Kim, true. Sheep were dying everywhere, and we were climbing up the trees and cutting the branches off, and raking all the sheoak leaves to feed the sheep and that.

While we there at Carney's another Noongar family came. Dad's cousin Sandy Mindum and his family came and stayed about five miles away. We used to see them on weekends. One weekend Dad took us all to a place called Mininyup, and he showed us the old grave sites there. There was two, three old people's graves there. We put pickle bottles there, you know. It was September, so there was lots of everlastings. And we put everlastings there, me and Aunty Maggie.

And it was funny, the year after that we found out that was the same place an old man called Noidi was buried. We didn't know that was where he was buried. We was too young to remember when Granny Mindum was buried there, because we weren't allowed to go to the actual burial places. Dad showed us different graves; they put stones on 'em to mark 'em, you know.

If work was scarce at the farm, well then mostly we travelled around, and we'd be hunting. We had two kangaroo dogs, and we'd go around to different waterholes and stay at different places; sometimes it might be a government dam on the side of the road, or sometimes a waterhole.

We used to go camping out there, stay there for about a week. Till they shoot all the kangaroos out, and then light a fire behind, like to burn all the scrub where they hunting, and then shift further down to another waterhole.

That's how we came to be familiar with the bush, and Dad'd show us middens and old camping places where they used to go and hide from the police when they were kids, old camp sites and places where something happened that was significant to them.

But now all that area around the Jerramungup area and around the Needilup area, everything is all changed now. When we were children, there was only thirteen families in the district altogether. Now really everything is all changed Kimmy, because since the Land Settlement, that farm business you know, all those places are in different sections now, and they're all fenced. It's sad really, you know. Middens, lots of camping sites, gone. All that's left is waterholes and grave sites.

You know our people are the last people to do a bush burial? Our people, we're the last people to do a bush burial. Everybody else went to Gnowangerup to be buried.

There's one lot of graves at Cherriderup, a lot of graves at Jerramungup, there's graves down at Quaalup, there's graves at Carney's, there's graves at Ongerup, and our grandmother's grave is over at Pingimup.

There's lots of graves because the people, you know, when they got dissatisfied with Hassell or whoever, most of them moved away from the station, or were shifted and went back bush.

Sometimes we used to all meet at Needilup Hall there, all our family. Uncle Malcolm was working at King's. Uncles and aunties. Uncle Bob Roberts, he came and stayed with us too.

Aunty Ellie and Uncle Dongup were down at Quaalup working while we were at Needilup. They went over to

Wellstead working up and down that area, you know. One of Dad's brothers was working way down at Hay River, and he came back home to us. I was about eight when he came to Needilup for Christmas.

Another of Dad's brothers and his wife stayed about five miles from us, working for a Mr Dave King. They had two children, my uncle and his wife. A little girl Daisy and a baby boy called Doust. This would have been about 1934.

Doust got sick one day and his mum and dad brought the two children over to our camp. The little boy was very sick and my dad made a big fire in the front of our tent. Mum nursed the baby in her arms and four o'clock in the morning the baby died. Medicine was very hard to get those days and we didn't have transport so the women did the best they could.

After the sun had risen my dad went up to the farmhouse and told Mr Brown what happened. Mr Brown got into his old car and drove over to the Pococks and from there he rang up the police in Gnowangerup. When he came back he brought some of the Mindums across to our place and Mr Pocock brought the rest of the family. They told Mr King what had happened and all the King family came over and brought food and flowers.

The men dug a grave about half a mile away from our camp under a sheoak tree near a spot where our grandparents camped years before. It was a lovely sunny day, and such a lovely spot. Everlasting flowers were everywhere. My aunt and uncle stayed with us for about a week and after that they left the district to go back to Aunty Connie's brothers who lived in Mount Barker.

I used to visit Doust's grave nearly every day and sit there for hours on end. I planted some freesia bulbs there and a geranium plant that my mum had got from Mrs Sparks. After that we never saw anyone else but the Mindums and it wasn't until 1936 that we saw our aunty and uncle again.

Me and my brother Lenny were reared up tough. We lost our own dad when we were only small, and we learned to be tough, you know. We never used to cry and feel sorry for ourselves. We missed out, but we never let other people see our tears.

That's how we were steeled. We learned how to be self-sufficient. We learned about hunting, about snaring, about tracking, and when we lived in the Jerramungup–Needilup district, I think me and Lenny would have known just about every mallee hen nest from Pingrup right back to Boxwood Hill.

There's a lot of our places that have been destroyed by white people, by farms and things like that. But the waterholes and some of our places are still there. And I always say, they can destroy our country but they can never destroy the memories of it. They can change it, but they can't change what we know about it, you know.

Me and Lenny wanted to go back and show our children. Take our kids back and show them where we grew up. Lenny's children have never been there.

The rest of the family never lived like we lived. They weren't shown what we were shown. So I think we had the advantage over them.

Lenny was funny. Every time we ever met any white people, or white people came to the farm, he used to say, 'Oh we're Aboriginal, we're Noongars, I'm a black boy.'

When we were growing up they used to get the *Western Mail*, and they used to have a cartoon of a little Aboriginal boy. The funnies. This Noongar that they used to draw, his name was George Commonwealth. Lenny used to always say, 'I'm George Commonwealth of Australia Brown.'

These fellas came in this big flash car. We were talking and eating gum, and we were that dirty — run out of soap, see. We were walking to Ongerup. There was Mary Woods, Ethel Woods, Johnny Woods, Jimmy Woods, Lenny, me, and Mavis Penny. Seven of us.

Mummy and Granny come behind in the cart, everything all packed on this dray, see. Old horse, he walking that slow.

We was coming up the hill at Warperup — there wasn't a bridge there then, used to just be a culvert — and just as we got on the rise we met this man and woman; old Chev car, canvas top, big high wheels.

Uh-oh! Everybody all standing. Wadjela got out, stopped, we met her on the side of the road. 'Hello, where you going?' Lenny said.

Lenny giving them the lowdown. Lenny, like he's the main talker, telling them everything.

Old girl said, 'Can we take your photograph?'

Lenny said, 'Yes. You take our photograph, but you gotta give us money. You gotta pay us.'

Wadjela says, 'Oh yes,' took all the photos; oh, everybody all posing. Wadjela give us a penny, give all the boys lollies. Next minute we're walking again, on our way again.

We get to Ongerup, and everybody comes up to us, and oh, they want to go to the shop. We got money, see.

'No,' old fella says, 'You're not going to shop, you're too

dirty to go to the shop. Gotta have a wash first.'

So we chuck the soap in — someone got some soap — throw the water around.

'Where'd you get the money from anyways?'

'Oh, wadjela give us money.'

'What they give you fellas, you never been cadging for money?'

'No,' Lenny said. 'They took all our photos. They're going to put us in the *Western Mail*.'

'Oh,' Grandfather Jack said, 'you reckon they put you in the *Western Mail!* They're gunna put you all in a settlement called Mogumber, that's where you're gunna be going. They might be welfare people,' he said. 'You fellas gunna be finished now.'

Well, one night in Ongerup there, and early next morning we packed up and headed straight to Needilup, went out into the bush, and stayed out in the bush for three months, never come back.

Old Granny said, 'I thought you had more sense. When you see wadjelas coming you gotta go and run and hide. You can't go up to them brave way.'

After that every car that came into the district, and there weren't many, we'd run. We knew the sound of all the Ford trucks in the district, we knew the sound, we memorised the sound. Any motor, when a man come around, come around for tax, taxation business, or wool buyers or anything like that … we be gone like bullets. They never see us, we be hiding in the bush. Never, never showed us off.

Not many wadjela can say that they ever saw any of us in the Needilup district.

But we met some other white people one day. We were coming back from Jerramungup. Sometimes Dad used to go down for supplies. We got some turkey eggs and whatever.

On the way back we met these people, they were going to Esperance. We were walking in the front, and Mummy and Aunty Evelyn and Grandfather Moses were coming behind in the sulky. Dad was riding the horse, way up ahead. This was near where Jerramungup townsite is now.

Now these people come along. They had an old black motor and I don't know ... it was like a square top and it had a funny little front. It was like a little ute. The funny thing was it had tin in front, and the back was all wood, bolted on. There was a woman and a man and a teenage boy. I can't remember what the numberplate was. Anyway, they pulled up and Lenny was at the front with me.

'Hello,' they said.

And Lenny said, 'Hello.'

And she said something, and he said, 'We're Noongars.'

And of course she wouldn't know what the word Noongar meant. And she said, 'Oh, what's a Noongar?'

He said, 'An Aboriginal.' He said, 'I'm black.'

He didn't have to tell her that because he looked black.

She said to him, 'Oh, what's your name?'

And he said, 'I can't tell you. I mustn't tell you.'

She said, 'Why?'

He said, 'You'll go back and you'll tell that Aboriginal Natives Department, and they'll come and get me and take me away.'

She said, 'No I won't.'

And then she asked me, like, you know, what my name was.

I didn't want to say anything to her, so I kept stalling for time and then Mummy came up.

She was very friendly. She was a woman that was going through to Esperance, and she was going to South Australia, and in some way she was connected to Daisy Bates. Dunno whether she was doing the work that Daisy Bates was doing or not. Anyway, she asked Mummy what was her address and that and then she started sending Mummy the little magazine that Daisy Bates made.

We got them monthly. She was very nice and very friendly. Mummy told her all about the Aborigines Department, and where she came from. The woman said that they'd be in Perth. Didn't mention that they were doing a survey and looking around for Aboriginal people, but she said they were travelling to Esperance 'cause they had family there.

Working country girl

Around 1939 I had to choose: go to Carrolup, or go to work. So I chose to go to work. I was fourteen years of age then. They sent me away to work for a Mr and Mrs Roy Wilhelm. They owned a store in Woodanilling. Little old house and a little old store, it stood on the corner and it's there now. I stayed at Woodanilling for six months. I worked in the house, domestic work. And I worked in the store too, measuring things and selling and that.

Fancy, if I'd saved up my money I'd be rich. I got two shillings a week for working down there.

The girl that I worked with — Mrs Wilhelm — she used to go to school at Carrolup with my mother. She knew my mother. Her maiden name was Schubert, and Schubert is one of the oldest white families in that district. She treated me just like I was one of the family, and nobody said anything about colour. I lived in the house. You know, I really liked those people; they had three children.

And then my mother got sick and I had to go back and

look after my little sister and brothers. Stanley and Aubrey were only small, and they went to school. I looked after Audrey and Lomas. Lomas was about six months old.

Mummy was in the hospital for three months. I used to walk down to the hospital every day. It must've been about four miles. I'd take Lomas down to Mummy for a drink of milk. I'd stay down there and come back about three o'clock in the afternoon.

Daddy used to work around the district. Sometimes he used to ride the pushbike out, and he'd always come back at night. Well, pushbike was the only way of travelling.

When Mummy was better — it musta been near the end of 1939 — I went out to the Richardsons. They're one of the real oldest families down in the Gnowangerup district. But it was different down there. I used to like going home on Sundays because I liked going to church. And all the family were back on the mission and I used to love to go home to my family. And I missed them, and I used to get lonely too. Mrs Richardson was always telling me, 'Oh, you don't want to go back every week.' She says, 'You want to try and forget those people. You want to try and make something of your life.'

'Look,' I said, 'if I can only make something of my life by staying away from my people, I don't want it. I don't want a life without my family. Without my mother, or my black father, or my black relations, because life wouldn't have any meaning at all for me.'

I was fifteen years of age then. I stayed at the Richardsons for twelve months. It was nearly 1941 when I left and went to work at MacDonald's. I stayed there for a few months, doing all sorts of work. I might've been called a domestic, but I did plenty of farm work too. They went away on holiday and left me to look after the farm on my own.

*

Some of Kayang Hazel's social history and anecdotes in these chapters are based on transcripts of interviews she did with Christine Birdsall-Jones in, I believe, the early 1980s. It was different times then, and her words may seem a little different in tone.

Most of her stories, however, I taped — sometimes several times and in various circumstances — and as I wrote them out I realised how polished several of them were. She'd told them many times; they were rehearsed. There was all that dialogue for one thing, recalled confidently and without hesitation. She did different voices, used a lot of body language. Sometimes she mimed the actions, or — by way of characterisation — took a few steps to demonstrate how someone walked. If there were other people with us this performance aspect of her stories drew them closer. Sometimes they'd provide their own embellishments, or even take over the story altogether and in this way a few people might end up telling the one story.

I thought I could see themes developing; the value of working hard, especially as a unit; Kayang standing up to white authorities in her feisty way and arguing them down; and racism, of course.

The refusal to separate herself from her family and her people, despite the pressure to do so, is a very strong thread through many of her narratives.

It was clear that some of these stories were ones she'd told to an audience of family, or at least to an audience of Noongars. But they weren't always about race or community solidarity, and often they were about someone — her — protecting the vulnerable and standing up to those who were, in one way or another, bullies.

I started tractor-driving when I was about eighteen. This was at Jim Bunjee's. We used to call him 'Squire'. I had my first tractor given to me to drive, and it was a crawler, boy.

Sometimes it was difficult. By now I had my first baby, and at first I took my baby with me, but then Squire's missus took the baby. So I was sitting down driving a crawler tractor. I did the big paddock, and to make sure I did it all I wouldn't cut it off in sections, I'd go right around. One thousand acres, whatever it was. I'd have a cowboy book on my lap. I'd be reading Zane Grey.

First tractor I ever drove was the crawler, then I graduated to the old Field Marshall — the old Pom-pom. Then we went for some diesel, and the last tractor I drove was a big Champ — a Champion — pulling two ploughs.

Most women wouldn't know how to drive a tractor.

When we was at Stone's, old boy — my husband, Harry Trumby Brown — was in the hospital up here in Perth, and so I did the scarifying — using the tractor to loosen up the ground — for the feed. Me and Philip Stone used to work together. Boondi Stone was the farmer, and Philip was his son. Philip was my good mate. I haven't seen him for a long time.

I pulled two scarifiers, and Philip filled the boxes up for me, you know. He put in the super, and I put in the seed. Me and him worked in the same paddock, two tractors. He pulled the great big plough with the big rake at the back, I pulled the two scarifiers.

When you worked on a farm years ago you had to fuel up, put water in, put in the kerosene or diesel or whatever it ran on. You do so many acres, and you'd have to stop and fuel up and then fill up the seed boxes, and of course you had to grease up the machinery and things like that, and after so many acres you'd have to change the tines of the scarifier — those little things that go in the ground like that — and if you lost any of them you'd have to replace them.

I remember old Boondi Stone; when Philip was about fourteen, Boondi was sick, or supposed to be sick. He was all make-believe, he was sick all the time. Every time work began, he got sick. He'd suddenly have a temperature, and run to missus for a needle.

He had blood pressure or something. Diabetes? I dunno. She giving him injections to quieten him down, supposed to have a bad heart. Funny bloody thing is, cancer killed him. Wasn't his heart that killed him.

He come down there one day, busting himself. Philip was down from boarding school see, come down from up there at boarding school.

'What the bloody hell you doing?' Boondi shouted. 'You can't do anything much, you bloody idiots,' and all this. 'Why you never got started …'

See, what happened is mallee roots got stuck in the scarifier and the tines snapped off. Going along fast, bump bump bump … Well, they broke.

So then we had to get the crescent spanner, we didn't have a ring spanner. Oh, looking everywhere for spanners we was, and all the tools somewhere way out in the paddock. We were down home, working near the house.

Anyway, we found this big wrench, and we found two new tines and we put them back. Just tightened it up, tighten it with the wrench. Big wrench, too.

And then Boondi come along. 'You bloody idiot!' And, well, Philip, he's a very soft-hearted boy, you know. Just like butter, you only had to touch him and he'd melt.

I said, 'Go on, leave him alone.' I was getting sick of it already. 'Go away you old bully, go on …'

And he's going off, 'Blah blah blah,' you know. He says, 'You know who you're talking to?'

'Yes, I know who I'm talking to,' I said. 'I'm talking to a bloke called Alan Stone, Noongars call him Boondi. I got a better name for him, but I don't want to offend him,' I said.

'You know what, old man,' I said, 'you come and bust yourself, order people around. You think you're King George sitting there with a crown on your head. You think just because we're working for you, you can blow your top whenever you want to.'

I said, 'I don't have to work for you, so don't you be ungrateful. This is your son, he's only a kid. I worked with Jim Bunjee's boys when they were only fourteen years of age, and I never ever heard the squire be abusive towards his children, and talk like you. You ought to be thankful that people are helping you.'

I said, 'You're supposed to be a sick man. If you so sick, what the bloody hell you doing here giving orders?'

Then Philip starts crying.

'Look,' I said to Boondi, 'you better go away. If you don't go away, I'll …'

But he kept on talking.

'Oh here you are,' I said. 'If you keep on busting yourself, do it your bloody self!' and I just threw the spanner, and he cocked his leg trying to dodge. You wouldn't believe it. Spanner broke his ankle.

Big wrench.

Cut him.

'Oooh.' Big fella. He had the flu, too, sniffing and that.

Got in the car, and he drove flat out down to the house.

'Come on Philip,' I said, 'He's an ungrateful old thing. When you grow up, don't have the farm. Let the old bastard have it for himself. You go and get yourself a good job, go and work for someone. Don't work for him. He's not satisfied with what anyone do for him. We worked for him now for three years, nothing we do can please him.'

Missus, she come to me. 'Oh, what's been going on?' she said. 'The boss come down, he was very upset,' she said. 'I thought he was gunna have a heart attack.'

I said, 'Well, I wish to God he had've had a heart attack, and dropped over dead. You might miss him,' I said, 'but I won't. The way he treats his boys, I doubt very much if they'll miss him either.

'Now listen, Mrs,' I said, 'he wants to get your ploughing done, the boys are ready to seed, and we're willing to do it. See, somebody else break something, and we're trying to fix it, get it ready to use. Not this little boy's fault. It's not my fault. It's your manager's fault. Some manager you got.

'The way you fellas treat him, you think he's someone special. But I don't have to work and take shit from your manager, or Boondi, or you either. I can just jump in my ute, I can go straight over to Mary and Graham's,' I said.

'I left a good job to come help you fellas out. I don't have to work for this old skinflint. You tell him, if he don't want to have a heart attack, to stay away from me. Don't come near me, the mood I'm in.'

Alan Boondi Stone was one of the old white men in Borden. His family started the first farm, this side of Borden. Old Joe Stone was his great-grandfather.

And the way Boondi'd talk — 'Mister this' and 'Mister that' — I tell you, that mister got paralytic drunk once, down in Borden.

I was down there at Mummy's. We were staying on the hill, and Mummy was doing my washing, and I seen Boondi's ute come in at about nine o'clock in the morning.

I said, 'Harry, I reckon the old man must be sick.' Harry come in about half past three. I said, 'That ute's been there since about nine o'clock. You better go and see, he might be sick.'

So Harry went in there to the pub, see. Alan Stone sitting up there on a stool, just about rocking and riding and drinking whisky. Whisky.

They tanking him up properly, all the boys, laughing. No police, see. No police.

Neville Moir laughing his head off, and Kevin Miller too. 'Oh, Harry Brown come, Harry Brown come to check the boss out.'

'Look at the state of him. The boss …'

'Oh, take me …' says Boondi.

Harry said, 'What you been doing here, old boy?' He said, 'I rang up the missus to ask where you was. I'm going out to get a killer. And she said she didn't know where you was. What's the matter with you, you're not drunk are you?'

'Oh, take me home.' He had a real toffee accent, Alan Stone.

Eric on one side and Harry on the other, they put him in the motorcar, and he just slumped right down, vomiting. I was driving. I pulled up to the phone box at the post office, and I rang up his missus.

I said, 'Missus.' I said it very sweetly, very sweet voice, you know. I wanted to get back at him, see.

I said, 'Missus, it's Hazel.'

'Oh hello Hazel. You haven't seen the boss have you?'

'Oh, he's paralytic drunk. We're just bringing him home now, in the ute. He's in a terrible state. You better meet him with the medication, he might need it.'

When we drive in he's going, 'Don't tell Nell, don't tell Nell.'

'Oh look, here's Nell now!' I say.

He couldn't talk. Choking. He was choking. His face was red as a cherry. And missus walked up.

'Just look at you. You ought to be ashamed of yourself.'

'Yeah, just look at him,' I said. 'Paralytic drunk! Just fancy,' I said. 'Everybody be talking about him in Borden now. Even the birds'll be singing this song.'

He was always preaching about drunken Noongars, see, and drunken people and that.

I've always stood up, I've always told it how it is. Say it straight you know, even when people don't like it. Sometimes you have to do it a different way too, if someone thinks they're so high-and-mighty special. It hasn't always won me a lot of friends. But I'm honest with my words, and I'm honest with my work. Not just me, my family know how to work, too.

'Cause Harry, my husband, he used to get sick too, you know. So my kids sat down and drove a tractor, Saturdays and

Sundays, and practically every day of the week for three dollars a day. They were on school holidays.

They'd start seven o'clock of the morning, and knock off at five o'clock. Or if they start at five o'clock they knock off at seven. My two teenage girls and my teenage boy worked for their school money you know. They used to fuel up, and water and grease up. They knew what to do, and the farmer'd go and check them out.

Elaine, and Mildred and James did that. Henry was only a little boy then.

See, even my kids've done a hell of a lot of work down there, and my husband and I, we used to have our own shearing team and do contract work. Get a team of men and go out and get a job and stay there until it was finished.

We used to go down to Bremer Bay, stay there for eight or nine weeks. I classed the wool, my husband looked after the machinery, and the shearers did their job.

A lot of the shearers were our own family, but I worked in mixed shearing teams too. White and black shearers. I remember watching and … well, the Aboriginal boys, they were too polite really, when you think about what it was like. They stood back, and let the white ones go out of the shed first.

One day we got talking about colour and races and all that. One bloke was only a teenager, and he was an Australian too. Well, he called himself an Australian but really his parents came out from England.

He said, 'You know, you coloured people have to bow down to us.' This is as true as God made apples and Jesus was nailed on the cross. And he said, 'We're your superiors. You have to listen to what I say.'

'Listen to me, my friend,' I said, 'your colour might be a slight bit different to mine, you might be one shade whiter, but me, I bow down to no-one.

'When I was a child, I took orders from my mother and father. I don't ever break the law. So the police always keep off my back.

'Matter of fact, I married an Aboriginal,' I said. 'I don't even bow down to my husband. I'm an open-minded person. I'm a free thinker and a free speaker. As for me bowing down to you, what can you do, that I can't do?

'All the years that I been working, taught by my parents to work, working amongst people, I can do anything that any man can do, rural work on a farm. I'd probably be able to shear a sheep. Because I know how it's done. I bow down to no-one.

'I take orders from the boss, but they don't treat me like dirt. I'll show you how one day.'

About four or five years later this boy came and worked in a shearing team where I was a boss.

I bossed that team. I was the wool classer. Yeah, I turned the tables on him, he took orders from me. When I was bossing a team, I never flaunted my authority. I just sort of explained to them what the boss expected us to do. And everybody went along with it and I didn't have any trouble but for that one smart alec that said we coloured people had to bow down to white people.

I told him, I said, 'Listen now, women won their rights a long time ago. One day, the black people are going to win their freedom too. I call no man master.'

It wasn't easy, not for any of us. A lot of the time there was no place even to sleep or cook. No accommodation, you know.

None of the white people, apart from Ian Duncan at Ongerup, ever built a cottage for the coloured people who worked on their farms. In the Borden district most farmers were the same. Oh, except at Jimmy Miller's, we lived in a shed and caravans. That's still my place now, I can go home there. They welcome me like family.

A lot of the time it was tents and bag huts. You got a job shearing, or clearing, or whatever it was, and you had to camp in the bush and drink dam water most of the time. The work was hard, the pay was low, and most of the white people treated you like dirt.

You did their shearing, you made your camp in the bush, you cooked your meals on an open fire. You carted water in buckets, carted firewood on your back. You were sometimes expected to shear wet sheep, and if you didn't you got the sack. And then you had to pack your camp and get back to wherever it was you come from as best you could.

Some of the Aboriginal men were working permanently on farms, and most of them camped with their families in tents or bag camps.

Most of the time the shearers in the district worked for much less money than the white men, and the shedhands — nearly all Aborigines — were underpaid too.

The Aboriginals didn't know about workers' unions so none of them ever joined, and none of the Native Welfare people ever bothered to tell them their rights. In the Borden district most of the workers would never complain because they were afraid it would cost them their jobs.

White men shear the sheep, they get to have cottages. Black man, you just go out there, chuck you in the scrub, pitch your tent. Pick you up Sunday night, Monday morning got to get on the board for work. That's why we give it up. That's why I moved to the city when I could.

One day I was in Perth, just after Noongars got their right to drink. Late sixties, early seventies must've been.

I wasn't an alcoholic; I used to *like* a drink. One of my dad's cousins was playing darts, and they were having a competition, and they got in the final. So of course we were all interested, we were skiting about what was gunna happen.

They were playing this other team that got in the finals too. It was Friday night, and they were all coming in. And that smart-alec shearer, the one who used to work with us, was walking in with them and me and him hit the doors together, and only one of the doors was open. He didn't even stand back; he thought, you know, that I was gunna give way to him. Me and him come side by side, and I walked through first.

He tapped me on the shoulder, and he said, 'Hey.'

I said, 'Hey what? That's in the paddock isn't it?'

'Hey,' he said, 'shouldn't you have let me go through first? I think that was quite rude. You should've let me go through first, shouldn't you?'

I said, 'No,' I said, 'Why should I?'

'Well,' he said, 'you Aboriginal people … you're Aboriginal?'

I said, 'Yes.'

He said, 'You call yourself Aboriginal, shouldn't you have waited for me to go first?'

I said, 'Why?'

He said, 'Well, I'm a white person, aren't I?'

And I said, 'Listen here mate, it's the principle, and it's respect. It's not about the colour of our skin. Seeing as how you're supposed to be a gentleman, even if you're a white one, and I'm supposed to be a lady, even if a black one, I was supposed to go before you. It was always taught to me as a child, the woman goes first, and the man comes after her. If you go into any pub, or any place, the woman goes first, even though the man is the leader, and the man is the boss.

'Aboriginal men,' I said, 'they respect their women. They let 'em go through first. If your mother taught you what life was about, then you should have been taught that a woman will precede a man. No matter what race, or the colour of their skin.'

I said, 'Long time ago, *this* woman was the boss for you, and you took orders from me. I never flaunted my authority, I treated you with respect, same as I treated all the others, and I was treated with respect, you know.'

I said, 'I hope there will never come a day when any white person expects me to walk behind them. I will listen to people, but the issue of black and white will never be a problem for me, because I think we're people; you're a person. I'm a person, no matter what the colour of our skin. You're not royalty and neither am I.'

I said, 'White people probably think I come from one of the lowest races on earth, but I think I'm equal to you any day ...'

And then, you know, the others all looked at him and said, 'Oh, shame on you.' But he only did it because he thought that he was being smart, you know, and being drunk at the time.

I got some good friends down the bush. I worked for a lot of farmers down there, and a lot of them I grew up with. My husband grew up with a lot of them too. And they accept me, they've been good to me, because if we did jobs, we did them properly. And people have helped me, and I've been a faithful servant to a lot of them too.

My bosses down there, their children call me Aunty Hazel. They all respect me. I call their fathers and mothers by name. And Gail and Peter Stone used to call me boss, and chief. They knew my father, my family, and we used to do the rounds, getting work where we could and staying away from towns until the season came, and then we went shearing and afterwards we went back to the bush.

I'd work for them and I was never underpaid. Other people underpaid their workers, but they didn't; not me, anyway. I dunno about anyone else. Gail and Peter were always grateful for the help you gave them. Peter would always say thank you — not like his cousin, old Boondi Stone — and give you a bonus and lots of other things. He trusted me. They could be away two to three weeks at a time, and know they could leave everything for me to take care of.

But there were other people down there that if they passed you on the street they'd pretend they didn't see you. Didn't matter if it was in Perth or Katanning or Albany.

Lots of times I've met up with Peter Stone. Peter picked his two kids up from school in Perth one day and I met him down there, and he put his arms round my neck and kissed me on the cheek and he waltzed me round. And the kids were that glad to see me too, and he says, 'Come on let's go and have a cuppa tea and a chat.'

So we walked up to Park Towers and we had a cuppa tea and we had a good old yarn. And we might all go down to the Show together, go look at everything; we might all go walk along the street and look in the shops, kid each other about the price of every little thing.

But there's a lot of people down there that wouldn't bid you the time of day. Oh, they think they above you in every way.

If God wanted one man to be boss of another man, well, he would've let 'em be born with crowns on their heads, now wouldn't he? God made everybody, black, white and brindle, and when you're born, you're not born with money. You're born of a woman, and most times you have a father to look after you. And you should be equal, but lots of people don't believe that. They don't believe it. You know, some might've been born into money. Born with a silver spoon in their mouth.

*

'It's all respect and being honest,' Kayang said to me many times, themes at the heart of so many of her anecdotes, those set pieces of hers. Respect and honesty.

I teased her about that once. I'd grown so familiar with her stories and I knew she didn't always tell them the same way. Sometimes she acted out the dialogue to such an extent that when I looked at the words separate from the performance I'd question if that was what she'd really said. And the dialogue of the same story would vary from one telling to another.

She clarified things for me.

'Everybody that was there is gunna tell it different, aren't they, Kim? And you know what a load of bullshit you get from some people; lies to protect themselves or their jobs, even if they're already big powerful people s'posed to be on top of things.

'Just 'cause something's written down doesn't mean it's true either, does it?'

No.

'I'm just telling it the way I saw it. That's all. I can tell you the way it *really* was, what it was about. Not all that "maybe-this-and-maybe-that" sort of thing.'

Oh.

'And Kimmy?'

Yes.

'We don't wanna bore people, unna? We wanna tell a good story. You should know that better than me, you s'posed to be the writer.'

Well, I know a story can be more true than the truth, and I know how a story can get to the very essence, the spirit of something. Especially when it's something like injustice, and the abuse of power.

Muddy dam water

I don't think that white people now, especially government people, I don't think they quite realise just how hard it was for Noongar people.

I remember I used to go and walk to Gnowangerup after school, and stay there, to comfort this little boy and look after that little boy, and then have to walk back.

When we came back from that hospital or anything, we had to walk across the paddock, true Kim. Police wouldn't let us take the road through the town. If they caught you on the road and asked you where you were going, you only had to say one or two words they didn't like, and then bang! They throw you into jail and you get a fine.

It was out of bounds for Noongars to be in town after six o'clock.

Even when people were living on the reserve, it was nothing for the police to drive round in the early hours of the morning.

The night we buried Mother, we sat up until the early hours. Had a fire at the reserve there, all sitting down yarning. There was a lot of people in town that day, they came from miles to Mum's funeral. And the police kept driving round and round and round.

You have to go down to the cemetery to bury your dead now. And the police, they'll always cruise up and down the road. Saying they're just looking for drunken drivers and unsafe vehicles. You can't even bury your dead in peace down there.

Down at my mother-in-law's funeral we were just walking near the cemetery in Gnowangerup. It was before they even brought the body along in the hearse. Her old husband didn't want to go to the church service, so I went down and waited with him at the gate. A traffic cop came past there twice, went up the road and came back again.

And just before we left the grave, my grand-daughters were very upset and I was talking, explaining things to them, just the family. And the police came. Came there in their van and drove past and came back. They just kept driving round. Wouldn't leave us alone.

Back when it was compulsory for boys to join the army they wanted extra men to send to Vietnam. They said, 'Oh, the Aboriginal boys should be conscripted, because this is their country.'

And I got up and I told them. I told them in the street, where they were talking about it. 'Now listen here,' I said. 'Fair's fair. No-one going to force my boys to join the army. What have they got to fight for? Who made the war in the first place?' I said, 'What country?'

And someone said, 'Well Australia's your country.'

I said, 'Yeah, big deal, eh?' I said, 'What we own in Western Australia is not worth laying down our lives for. Most of us only got the reserve, and even then we haven't got the title deeds for it. We don't bloody well own it, so why go and fight for them?'

I was talking to Vin MacDonald, a man I worked for, and he says to me, 'Look Hazel you know the trouble with your people is, your people are lazy. Most of them won't work.' He said, 'Army'll be good experience.'

Lazy! I looked after that man's farm for eleven months on my own while he was sick. I looked after his sheep myself, and the ewes were lambing. I fed eighty pigs, and milked cows, stayed at that farm by myself. Sixteen years of age I was.

The rams used to get out and people'd be ringing up, 'Oh, there's a couple rams in here, you got to come and get them.'

I couldn't drive a car, there was only an old dog cart. I spent half my time getting his crossbred rams out of other people's paddocks. Some brought them back. And you know, he never even bought me a handkerchief for that.

He said, 'There's a lot of boys running around here getting into mischief that should be in the army.'

Those days, we weren't allowed to drink. You had to have your citizen rights. And I said, 'Now listen here Mr MacDonald, you get this straight from me. If you think Gnowangerup is worth fighting for — if you want people fighting for your town, well, then you should've helped make it a town that's been good to us.'

I said, 'Look, I was in Perth, and, oh one Aboriginal boy, Ronny Harris, he got shot over there, his mate shot him accidentally.'

My mum's cousin was the mother of that boy, Ronnie Harris.

And one white woman came along and she says, 'Oh, but don't you reckon that he was a brave boy? He went away to fight for his country, he gave his life for his country.'

I said, 'Gave his life for what? What did he give his life for?' I said, 'What's his wife going to gain?' I said, 'What will his mother ever have?' I said, 'They say you're brave, they give you a medal. So what?' And I said, 'I'd rather they got shot like my brother got shot. Out having a bit of fun chasing a kangaroo. Them who go and get shot over there are fighting people they don't know, that they've never heard of.' I've seen five men go away from down Gnowangerup, Katanning district. They went away to the army, one was a prisoner of war. And that was Arthur Morrison, Freddy Eades, one other Eades, old Jack Coyne and Freddy Punch. They been Palestine, everywhere.

I just walked away, because some of them Noongars came back with malaria, and some came back alcoholic wrecks, but when they came home they couldn't even get served a drink in the hotel.

When they died they never even had a military funeral for them. They're lying in unmarked graves. They never got help from the Repatriation Department; it never set them up with farms. No Land Settlement Scheme for them. Jerramungup's all Land Settlement, but the black man, he got nothing. Not a thing. They didn't recognise them.

Gnowangerup has always been like that. You go on a football field, Aboriginal boys down there, the best footballers in the district. They all mates on the football field. But when the game is finished, the white man go into the clubroom, or into the pub, to have his drink. The black man has his bottle underneath a tree or in the car.

You couldn't drink in the pub down at Gnowangerup. Woman couldn't go and sit down in the lounge and have a drink. You bought your bottles from a little place on the side. You went there, and you bought your bottles, and you drink them in the street, or more likely at somebody's place, or in the bush. You didn't get served a drink in there. At least not many people did.

One boy from Queensland, Freddy Hardy, he had a white father and Aboriginal mother. His father, Uncle Tom, was living not far from the reserve in one of the old state houses and he took Freddy into the pub. They said, 'We'll serve you Tom, but we can't serve him.'

Tom said, 'He's my son.'

'Oh,' they said, 'he's still an Aboriginal.'

So, the old boy told them to shove it and he walked outside. Freddy was in uniform; he been in Queensland in the army for two and a half years and just come back. That's how they are.

Down there in Gnowangerup, you couldn't go into the cafe and have a meal. You wouldn't get served a meal at the table. No way in the world. If you wanted to buy a meal, you might be able to eat it outside. But you'd never eat in there.

It wasn't much different in Borden when time come for me and Harry to send our kiddies to school. We was working on a farm, living there, and my husband used to have to drive them the nine mile into town.

Our kiddies wanted to go to school, and they went to school in Borden and Gnowangerup as we moved about working on different farms, but things got harder as they got older. There always used to be trouble. Farmers' kiddies used to be cheeky. Call 'em 'little black sambos'. My kids used to be called 'the black Browns'.

Olive and Eric came home from school one day talking about the 'colour bar' at the school. See, when it was interschool sports and that, the little kids could go in and have afternoon tea but the mothers couldn't, just because they were black.

When one of kiddies said, 'Oh why didn't they come and have a cup of tea, Mum?' Someone said, 'Oh, that's a colour-bar town.'

And my little girl, Olive, she asked, 'Well, what's colour bar?' She come back and asked me, 'What's colour bar, Mummy?'

I looked at her. I worried what was going on in her head. I said, 'Why do you want to know?'

She said, 'I want to know because the kids are talking about it at school.'

Eric was very smart for a ten year old; he spoke up and said, 'Oh, colour bar means that we're black and the white kids are white.' He said, 'The law say that black people can't go where white people can go. That's how black people get put in jail if they have a drink, because they're not allowed to, they're *barred* from drinking.'

'Well, that's funny,' she said, 'I'm black and we're people aren't we?' and she says, 'They're always talking about colour, I hate the way they're always talking about colour, I hate that school.'

There was trouble at school, there was trouble in town. Trouble everywhere.

You know me, I got a big mouth and a long tongue. Oh, maybe I just wanted to make myself heard, and maybe I just wanted people to think that I was really somebody.

But I had seen how people had been put down for years. And I knew that there was a lot that could be done, you know? And I was damn sure that they needed help, and so I spoke up. Didn't matter where I was.

At Borden Reserve people had to get water from a dirty old dam. The dam would've been, oh, maybe a couple of metres wide and not much longer. It was that muddy; more like muddy cream than water. Nearly *all* the families was camped there.

Me and Harry was living at the railway. They built three houses there, and Harry was working for the railway then. We was in one, Dudley Pickett was in one, and Stanley and See-wee was in the other one. There were two water tanks. We shifted there in the winter time, and then a bit of a rain come, and one tank was about half full, and the other was just about full — we had the guttering and tin roof, see.

Down at the reserve kids kept on getting sick. That's why we shifted. Five babies died while I was there. Five babies died. Bonnie and Gerald lost their baby, and Sam. Aunty Tilda lost her little baby, Lenny and Iris lost their baby, Aunty Joyce Cockle I think lost a baby. There was five from the Borden district.

They was getting this dam water all the time, see. The water was that muddy and in the summer, to purify it, the women used to have to cart a bucket of water and throw the ashes from their fires in it and that would clear it. Then Noongars started getting water from the tanks at the goods shed. So then the town put locks on the tanks at the railway station and there was a notice: you weren't allowed to get water from there, you had to get it from dams.

Well, then I said to them, 'You fellas might as well shift, and get water from us.' Otherwise all they could do was steal water from the soak there, on the farm.

Some of them shifted, others wouldn't. Or couldn't. They weren't welcome, you know. So, anyways, after all these babies been dying, I wrote a letter to the State Health Department in Perth. I wrote a letter to the premier of the state, and the Aboriginal Affairs Department. And I wrote a letter to a good old doctor who'd looked after Lizzie and Henry for me, when they had rheumatic fever. No lie, I got John Tonkin, old Kim Beazley, Mr Garrison, and members of the Roads Board. About seven or eight people. This was around 1957, before we got the big flood.

They sent me a telegraph. Said that they'd organised for us to have a meeting, and to organise all the Noongars.

So, we went out to the reserve. Daddy come up, Cedric was there, Lenny was there, Aubrey was there. All the Pennys was there, and Dudley and Monica, Lionel and Mari, and Aunty Esta and all the Woods. Oh, about thirty or forty Noongars, you know, like the elder ones.

We were introduced to them. I'd met Mr Beazley before; I'd met him in Perth. We shook hands. The shire was there: three or four blokes. Mr Norrish was there, Keith Davis was there, Neville Moir was there, and I think Kevin Miller could've been there. All the members of the shire, Gnowangerup shire. Couple of justices of the peace. We had Mr Webster from Narrogin, we had Aboriginal Affairs from Gnowangerup.

Beazley said, 'What's the real reason the children been

getting so sick and are dying?' and he asked if we'd been seeking medical help.

And I said, 'Well, we were the only ones with a motor, see. Me and Harry. And the babies get sick.' Harry was always running them to and forth. 'We been taking them to doctor, and sometimes he'll see them and sometimes he won't.'

It was a hot summer, very, very hot. And the flies. We had no protection from flies. Not even at the railway, where we were.

And Beazley said, 'What's the water like?'

And I said, 'That's the reason I wrote you the letter. I think this dam is diseased. Everybody wants citizenship rights. They want the right to drink. But what we need for our people is water. We need clean drinking water above all things. Because water,' I said, 'you can't live without it.'

Well we got in all the motors, eleven cars there were, and we went to the reserve.

'Where's the dam?' Beazley said.

I said. 'This here is what they call a dam. What would you call it? This here is an Aboriginal reserve. And these people — the Aboriginal Affairs Department and the shire — they're the bosses of this reserve.'

I said, 'Who's responsible for the health of the people? We got no houses. They got no tin roof to collect the water. I shared water with 'em. Harry carted soak water in, to do washing and that. Carted water from some of the farms. Boss lent him a truck on the weekend. My husband is working on the railway, but he makes it his business to try to get drinking water for them. Water is something that they need.'

Beazley said, 'This isn't a dam. This is just a pothole.'

'Well,' I said, 'you see all those cowpats there? The cows use this water too. When the white men bring his cows here, he bring his dogs with him too, and they swim. Or try to, when it's got more water than this of course. I seen one bloke, Charlie Travis, lying in this dam once. I seen Travis woman in it too.

'You see that green caravan over there? He's a dam-sinking contractor. Matter of fact,' I said, 'he's just about on his way now to go to Jerramungup. Get that bulldozer on that lowloader and they're going out to the Land Settlement. They're going out there to do a dam.'

Beazley said, 'Go and ask him if he'll put a dam here.' And he said, 'Has he got anyone to help him?'

Lenny said, 'Yeah, I'll help him. I'll help him.' Lenny and him — Keith Green it was — been doing contract work together.

Lenny went over there, and big fella came back with him. He was a good boy too.

'We want to put a dam down here,' Beazley said. 'Could you put a dam down here?'

'Yeah, I could put a dam down here,' he said. 'These people need water.'

'The moment you finish it,' Beazley said, 'there'll be a cheque in the bank for you. The money,' he said, 'is coming from the Gnowangerup shire.'

Lenny grabbed an axe and started cutting sticks; making pegs, see. Contractor came back. He said, 'We'll have this ready in two or three days.' There were two dozers.

They marked it out with the sticks Lenny had cut. Taped it all, him and Lenny. Harry could drive a bulldozer too, so him and the contractor were working in there, one going one way, the other going other way, boy. And them two big dozers just missing one another.

Two and a half days. And while they're doing that, Lenny got on the caterpillar tractor and cut a big drain.

And you know what, boy? God must've been wanting to help the Noongar people — something must've been wanting to help — powers up above, or might've been our old people.

I'm hanging the clothes out on the line now, and looking at the clouds. I knew they were just finishing off the dam. 'Only gotta wait for the rain to come,' everyone was saying. 'We'll get our water.'

'Well, the only way you gunna get water in that dam,' I said, 'is you go kill a *kalari* — you know, yellow-tongued lizard — and skin it. That's what Ralphy and me did, years ago, when we made a big flood at Gnowangerup. Ralphy Woods. If we could do it then, you can do it now,' I said. 'Go find a kalari and skin it, and it'll rain.'

I looked towards the hills and you could see these white clouds, just like ice-cream. And down at the bottom was black.

And just when they took the last load of sand out, it started raining. Rained for two days and two nights, and when we went to have a look at the dam, it was just about overflowing. Water was everywhere, and everybody all smiling. They were that pleased. Matter of fact, it rained that much that our two tanks overflowed. Danny and them's tanks overflowed, and the big tank overflowed; I tell you what, we had our water.

That was a miracle, you know. That was the reason why so many little children always got sick. They didn't have clean drinking water. Funny to think it now, how happy we were to get dam water. Dogs and anything could still drink from it.

Gnowangerup doctors

In the days before we had good doctors in Gnowangerup, the government didn't seem to care. Whether they wanted the black race to die out or what, I don't know, but they never helped. It was hard.

Going back to the very early 1920s, the people of Gnowangerup and surrounding district got very poor medical attention. Aboriginal people weren't allowed into the Gnowangerup Hospital, so when there was a bad outbreak of diphtheria amongst the camp people, a lot of them died.

Not that all the doctors were bad. Some were good.

There was a Dr Hanrahan in Gnowangerup in the late twenties and I been told he always came around and visited the sick people in the camps before and after his surgery hours. Our people weren't allowed to go into the white surgery for medical attention.

After Dr Hanrahan left, there was an elderly Dr Willing and

he did the same as Dr Hanrahan. When the flu epidemic hit in the 1930s most of the real old people died, and most of the little ones. Still the same; not one was allowed into the Gnowangerup Hospital.

If any needed surgery then Brother Wright took them to Dr Pope in Katanning. If any died they were buried in Katanning.

Then Gnowangerup District Hospital was built in the middle 1930s. The big building in front was for white people, and three wards about twenty or thirty yards back were for the Aboriginals; one each for men and women, and a ward for the children. The women weren't allowed into this hospital to have their babies.

Then a new doctor came to Gnowangerup, Dr Boyd. He would come out to the new mission nine miles out of town to help deliver the babies, all hours of the night.

Our family were back in Gnowangerup Mission for a while at this time and my mother Nellie Roberts, her cousin Mena Innell, and Sister Wright from the mission all helped with the birth of the babies.

Even when it was raining heavy they had to make a fire in the open and heat up the water that was needed to try to keep the mother and babies warm. They used to have the babies in a six by eight tent.

When there was a lot of whooping cough, measles, flu or other sickness, the real sick children were taken into the big hospital and kept in the isolation block. If there was too many patients then a big army marquee was pitched behind the hospital and beds were put in and the sick ones nursed there.

Dr Boyd was replaced by Dr Parton in the late 1940s. Dr Parton had no liking for dark people and was nearly always surly. He never came up to the mission as Dr Boyd did, and the people had to go into town to the surgery.

When you were sick you had to sit on the verandah of his house and wait until he treated his white patients. He didn't like you in his surgery; he examined kids down on the ground, or on the verandah, in the draught. No matter how sick, the Aboriginals had to wait until the very last. Always it was white before black in the early fifties.

One Monday in June 1951, I went into Gnowangerup at ten o'clock with my baby girl, Valda Glennis. She had taken sick suddenly and my husband and I made the trip some twenty miles or more to get help.

I went to Dr Parton's house, to the surgery, and knocked on the door. Mrs Parton came out. I told her that my baby was very sick and she needed help. Mrs Parton told me that her husband did not have surgery on Mondays. So I went up to the hospital where I saw the matron, Miss Formby, and asked her if she could please take my baby's temperature and then ring up the doctor or perhaps admit the baby.

'Oh, I can't keep her in the hospital if the doctor won't see her,' she said. 'You better take her home.'

You know I felt hatred towards that woman.

She said she was not permitted to put the baby in the hospital or do anything for or to her without Dr Parton's consent.

I was very upset and was eight months pregnant at the time and I knew in my own heart that my baby was very sick.

So my husband and I went back to the doctor's house. His car was in the garage and as I walked to the door of the house I saw the doctor standing in front of the window. I knocked, and the doctor's wife opened the door and said, 'Not you again.'

I said, 'Please tell the doctor I need his help for my child.'

She told me that Dr Parton was up at the golf links playing golf and to come back Tuesday morning.

We got into the car and went back to our camp at the farm. My husband left me there with the children and then drove into Borden about twenty miles away and brought back my mother.

Seven o'clock that night my little girl died in my arms.

I saw that he went to court. I made a lot of trouble for him. I rang up Merredin, the district supervisor and I told him I want this man shifted.

And there were some white people that backed me up on it. I took Dr Parton to court in Narrogin and he got banned from practising medicine.

Two days after court, he come along and chipped me in the street. I got out of the motor car.

'Thank you very much,' he said, 'for getting my job taken away from me. I'll probably end up like you,' he said. 'I'll have to pick mallee roots.'

I said, 'I couldn't care if you went and emptied shit buckets.'

He said, 'I lost my job.'

I said, 'I lost a child. And lots of others did too.'

Dr Parton was replaced by Dr MacCormick, who was very helpful to our people but still examined us on the verandah or in the waiting room. It was about this time coloured women were admitted to the hospital to have babies and we were all happy about this.

It was different after he came. He ran tests on the people and had them X-rayed and if they didn't seem all right he'd have them sent up to Royal Perth.

My cousin Harold had this bad knee. And then his glands became swollen. A lot of his family had died of TB. Could've been anything. I told Dr MacCormick, I said, 'Harold's got this bad knee, and his glands are swollen. You think you could see him?'

He said, 'You go and get him and bring him in.' So I went and I picked him up and I brought him in.

He examined him, and I told him, 'You know doctor,' I said, 'his mother died of TB; just about all the family on my dad's cousin's side died of this disease and there is a place in Perth where he can be helped.'

And he said, 'Too damn right there is Hazel. We'll get him there as soon as possible!'

So my husband came up to Perth; he brought Harold up on the train and he took him over to Bennett House and they took him straight out to that place and then he stayed there for two and a half years. And he was real good when he came back, you know.

At the end of the 1950s, Dr MacCormick left Gnowangerup and we were blessed with the presence of Dr Winrow, who treated us people like the scum of the earth and in one year alone about half a dozen babies died in infancy.

Hilda Penny took her little boy. Doctor said he wasn't very sick. The baby then died.

Shirley Wynne's baby died after seeing the doctor. He said, 'This child is really quite all right.'

Rita Wynne took her baby very sick. He would not admit this baby and later it died.

You'd think it was like they wanted to get rid of all the

Aboriginal people. Genocide in Gnowangerup. Go down there to Gnowangerup cemetery, and there's a row of little graves. Have I showed you them? In the line where Lenny and Cedric are, down the bottom there. A row of little graves, children who died within just five weeks of each other.

The town just about crucified poor Lenny and Iris when their little daughter died and they tried to get something done about it.

I was in the Albany hospital with a lung complaint when my brother Lenny's little daughter was put in the hospital at Gnowangerup. She died a few days later.

Dr Winrow was taken to court for Wilful Neglect, but he won. This wasn't the first time. Just about all the farmers turned against Lenny and Iris. At the court case nearly all the white people who backed Dr Winrow came along to support him. One Mr Tom Hart put a piece in the papers saying how the coloured women of the district — and my sister-in-law Iris Roberts in particular — neglected their children.

That was bullshit.

Everyone seemed to turn on us. White people at the court case were very hostile and that made Noongars scared. One of the reasons our people wouldn't speak out against this doctor was because they were afraid of violence.

After this, just a few months after the death of Iris and Lenny's baby, my brother Lomas and his wife Ruth took their baby to Gnowangerup Hospital from Ongerup. I went in with them. The baby had cut its finger very bad. The doctor was at the hospital this particular day and he said he would keep the baby in the hospital.

I went into the bathroom with Ruth and helped her bath

the baby and put pyjamas on him. Then Lomas and Ruth went back to Mr Foster's farm where Lomas was shearing, and every day for two weeks they rang the hospital.

Two weeks after the baby was put in the hospital the parents received a phone call from the hospital to say they could pick the baby up the next morning.

Early next morning they went into the Gnowangerup Hospital to collect the baby, only to be told by the matron the baby had died.

For over six weeks they had to wait while their child's body was sent to the Princess Margaret Hospital for examination, and after that it was sent over to the eastern states. They were never told what caused the death of their son and I don't think they know now what happened.

Dr Winrow was always well supported by the white community in Gnowangerup. If our people wanted proper medical attention they had to travel all the way to Albany or Katanning.

The doctors in Katanning and Albany were very disgusted with Dr Winrow's treatment of Noongar people. It was because of Dr Winrow and the white people's treatment of us that a lot of Noongars shifted to Albany — and most still live there today.

I myself had taken two of my children to Dr Winrow on two separate occasions. Each time I was given tablets and medicine and was told that they weren't very sick. Straight after seeing him I took my daughter to Katanning and she was admitted to the hospital with glandular fever.

After Dr Winrow diagnosed my son as 'not really sick' I

took him to Albany. He spent over three months in the hospital there with rheumatic fever.

It wasn't just children either. One of my sons, Henry Roberts Brown, was involved in a car accident in which his cousin was killed. Henry was the driver of the car. He was unconscious when picked up by the ambulance from Chillinup and taken to Gnowangerup. It was on the third of December 1971. Henry was, according to Dr Winrow, very drunk, and the doctor took blood samples for the RTA.

My son-in-law Roy Miniter and my daughter Elaine — Henry's elder sister — visited Henry in the hospital. While they were there they both spoke to the doctor. They asked what Henry's injuries were, and were told that he just had a few bruises. He was discharged three days later and was taken back to Borden to where he was living with his wife.

But after that he kept suffering with bad headaches and he couldn't move his neck, so his sister brought him up to Perth to where I was living at the time. They arrived at eleven o'clock at night and the next morning, the seventeenth of December, my husband and myself took him into Royal Perth Hospital by taxi.

I went straight to the casualty section and explained to the sister at the desk what happened and that my son was very sick. She went to the doctor and the sister brought a wheelchair and took my son to the examining room. The doctor soon told us that the X-rays showed that Henry had two broken vertebrae in his neck and his collarbone was fractured.

Within an hour of the doctor seeing him he was in the operating room. He had to have holes drilled in his skull and weights on his legs. He stayed in RPH until March.

If he hadn't been brought to Perth he would've been dead.

He went to court for Negligent Driving Causing Death.

Henry did six months in the Albany prison with a brace on the broken neck. We didn't know until it came out in court that there was a gutter in the road left by the machine that had just graded the road where he had the accident, but he was found guilty and went to jail while still under medical treatment.

None of our family ever visited Winrow's surgery after this incident.

An Angry Town

Gnowangerup: A tiny dossier of death threatens to turn this quiet rural town into an angry hotbed of racism.

People are afraid to talk now but the rippling undercurrent of resentment may soon become a tidal wave.

A hard core of people are hinging their prejudice on a recent court case.

The case involved the town's doctor Alec Winrow, who has been committed for trial at Albany on a charge of manslaughter of a native baby.

The town is angry and the issue is serving as a wedge to further segregate black and white human beings here.

Gnowangerup is the centre of the Great Southern's biggest native population.

The native reserve, hidden behind trees and scrub, contains about 300 Aboriginals — half-castes, full bloods, quarter castes the lot.

And the 750-strong white population doesn't like it.

The segregated cemetery here bears grim testimony to the relations between black and white.

But the locals greatly resent any attempt to appraise the situation.

Photographer Ian Harris and I had this welcome when we entered Gnowangerup service station this week:

'Get that bloody thing (our camera) out of here. We know what you're after. If the bloody thing goes off it won't get out of here in one piece.'

...

We were threatened with everything from smashing our equipment to a thump in the ear before we had a chance even to identify ourselves or state our business.

We visited the school, police departments, religious leaders and others.

The public servants as always hastily retreated into their little castles of anonymity relating to the old platitudes about being gagged and unable to say anything.

Everywhere else we plainly found people afraid to speak their minds.

And we also found an abundance of discrimination.

We were told a native was unable to sit in any of the town's cafes for a meal.

They are refused entry to the town's drive-in.

An official at the drive-in's canteen told us: 'They (the natives) ruined one business in town. Now we just don't have anything to do with them.'

But it was obvious to us that the aboriginal population of Gnowangerup is the mainstay and backdrop for the district's development.

While other districts are crippled by the nation-wide labour shortage an almost endless supply of labour is available in Gnowangerup.

Ace football umpire Tony Pitsikas agreed.

'When I came here sub-contracting I couldn't get men,' he said. 'The police arranged a couple of noongars for me. They are the best workers I ever had. On time every morning. Never drunk. Work hard all day long.

'I have sub-contracting work in Kojonup and Katanning after this and my boys will come with me. I couldn't have done without them.

'The only thing wrong here is that there is no electric light out on the reserve. What can kids and parents do by candlelight?'

Mr Pitsikas was almost overwhelming in his praise. We couldn't stop him.

Police sergeant Tom Dovey told us there was little trouble in the town. Virtually no drunkenness or other incidents.

The main trouble seems to be the white man's superiority complex and a great deal of apathy.

…

The most outstanding people we found toward the aborigines were two retired Baptist clergy, Brother and Sister Wright.

These two humble people have spent 40 years among the natives.

They are the confidants of the coloured people of Gnowangerup.

At all hours of the day and night they come to them and they help them.

However, they were too pleasant a couple to help us with the delicate task with which we had been assigned.

But they left me with the impression that their 40 years work had ben frustrated by white apathy and continual changes in government policy.

Probably their efforts have been negated to a degree by the hard core of whites who refuse to accept the black population.

…

Everywhere we went we found examples of discrimination — not a desperate situation but a grim threat to the future.

There is even talk of Gnowangerup people organising a demonstration at Dr Winrow's trial.

They should be big enough and old enough to know that they can not and should not try to interfere with the course of justice.

Albany Advertiser, *9 August 1965*

In the town of Gnowangerup there was always a colour bar. The government and different churches built nice homes for the fair-skinned Noongars, but the real full-bloods of the district, the old pensioners and the ones who had no close relations, were all sent away to a pensioners' home in Esperance.

Most of the people sent down to Esperance had been in the Gnowangerup and Borden–Ongerup area all their lives and most of their relations are buried in the Gnowangerup cemetery.

Uncle Sandy Mindum, who died in Esperance, lost all his family — he was one of the last of his family apart from one niece, Rita Allen, and two nephews, Richie and Dexter Williams. He was buried in the Esperance cemetery because his relations were pensioners and weren't able to bring his body back to Gnowangerup where all his brothers and sisters were buried.

The Mindums never got help from the Native Affairs Department. They looked after and reared their families themselves.

None of the Mindums ever went to school nor did any of the other children of the Ongerup district who were dark, because white people would never allow it. And if any white person lived in the Aboriginals' camp or had anything to do with the women, they were charged by the police. The so-called crime was punishable with a six-month sentence in the Fremantle prison then.

Racism was like law, it was official. That's what made it hard, but even then, even way back, not everyone was like that. My father had quite a few friends in the Ongerup and Needilup districts because he'd known some of them from his early boyhood days. Two brothers — Sid and Percy — used to bring us eggs, milk and fruit as they had a few fruit trees. They were good people and the colour of a black man's skin was not offensive to them.

And my own kids, they're black people, but they're fair-skinned, you know. Like my daughter Olive; to look at her you'd think, 'Oh, she hasn't got any coloured blood in her.'

Lots of people'd say that to her when she was working at the Trades and Labor Council. They'd say, 'Oh, where'd you come from?' She said to this one fella who asked her, 'I come from the bush.'

'What part of the bush?' he says.

'I come from down Gnowangerup way,' she says. 'I was born in Gnowangerup.'

'Oh,' he says, 'Gnowangerup. Yeah, I heard about that town.' He said, 'Are you Aboriginal?' He thought he was being funny.

She said, 'Yes, I'm an Aboriginal.'

He said, 'You are not an Aboriginal.'

She says, 'Course I'm an Aboriginal,' she said. 'I'm proud of it too.'

Lots of people, you know, were ashamed to admit that they got coloured blood in 'em. I don't think that, never thought it. No-one needs to be ashamed of their colour or where they come from, or what circumstances they were brought up in.

And that's what I really believe, you know? There's lots of people, they've been turned away from their own kind. You'll never make it in a white man's world, they say, if you cling to the blacks.

We didn't ask to be born, and we didn't ask white people to come here either. We had no choice. But colour is nothing to be ashamed of; people should be proud of their colour. They should be proud of their tradition. And our people's laws were really something. I'm not ashamed.

Lots of people say to me, when I been working, 'Oh, you shouldn't mix with this lot and you shouldn't mix with that lot.' When my husband and I got married, we went and lived on a farm. We didn't always live on the reserve.

But that didn't mean to say we didn't feel for our people, and that we didn't help them in any way we could. Because if there was ten people on one side of the street, and one black man on the other side of the street ... Well, I'll go to the black man's side any day.

Not because I got anything against white people. Some white people been really good, you know? And some people have helped all along the way. But there's people down in country towns, they're so small-minded, just because you got coloured blood in you. If you don't want to leave your people, well they tread them down and then they tread you down on top of them. You'll never make it in a white man's world, they say, if you cling to the blacks.

Lots of people, they've been turned from their own kind. Lots of people were ashamed to admit that they got coloured blood in them.

Stranded on a fault line

Write down the areas of society where Kayang Hazel has seen race make a difference; it's like listing government departments: Employment, Sport and Recreation, Education, Health, Water ... take it as evidence of institutionalised racism.

Experience like Kayang Hazel's — of how race has been used to divide people, and make them ashamed of themselves, their relations and heritage — is what creates the imperative to declare your Indigenous heritage and identity: you can't be bit and bit, you have to choose. Decide, one way or the other.

Kayang Hazel is particularly proud of her fair-skinned daughter telling people she's Aboriginal, because it means she's emphasising heritage, solidarity, and at the same time — given her appearance — subverting notions of exclusively race-based identity.

And when her father said Lenny didn't need to tell strangers he was black because they could see it for themselves, perhaps the implication was that, unlike Lenny, Kayang would need to tell them she was too — and that she should do so.

Lots of people, they've been turned away from their own kind. You'll never make it in a white man's world, they say, if you cling to the blacks.

I'd grown up knowing very few Noongar people to whom I was related, and they themselves knew little of connections into the Noongar community. Had we deliberately cut ourselves off from other Aboriginal family, or been isolated by the history and circumstances of our region? Whatever the answer — if there is one answer — Kayang's talk of country towns and the divisions between Noongar people had a very sharp edge.

Uncle Lomas — who's almost fifteen years younger than Kayang — drew me a map to show how a reserve he spent a lot of time on was divided by skin colour. He named people living in the different areas. We'd never see some of those fair people, he said. And if it's true that *no-one needs to be ashamed*, it's also true that plenty were encouraged to feel that way.

'He told his kids to marry white people,' I once heard someone say of an elder, and — it was long ago — I was still naive enough to wonder at their bitter tone. Stupidly, I didn't fully comprehend how skin colour was a way of dividing society, and how fairer skin advantaged you. The elder's instruction may have been motivated by shame, or simply by a pragmatic desire to help his children find a better life.

These days, you're more likely to hear fair-skinned Noongars say they want to marry someone really black, have really black kids. That's partly the result of a race-fixated history. Apparently most individuals in Afro-American society marry another of their 'own kind'. It's different here; sixty-five per cent of Australia's Indigenous people marry non-Indigenous people. You could say it's a continuation of traditional practice — exogamy — because it's certainly not a commitment to 'biological absorption'. Of course, fingers crossed, it might mean we're moving away from the racist polemics our society is founded upon, and that racism *hasn't* been fully internalised. I don't know what the figures say about the Noongar community but I think there's a feeling that it's best to 'marry black'. It makes sense that people feel that way, given the history and how it continues.

Myself, I married a non-Indigenous woman; specifically, to continue the clumsy appellations, an Irish-German immigrant.

One of my sons, five or so years old, fell asleep sobbing, 'How come I don't have black skin?' He'd had a long day in his short life, but I was shocked to find him hurting that way. My boys have been called 'boongs' and 'niggers', and they've also been called 'white cunts'.

They wouldn't get any of this if I hadn't accepted the political imperative to choose either Noongar or wadjela, and agreed that you can't say you're bit and bit, or 'part-Aboriginal', or 'of Aboriginal descent'. So, have my own psychological and political preoccupations — not to say spiritual inclinations — led my children into a 'no-man's-land', made them targets from either side of a social schism, a historical, racial fault line?

Have I stranded them where stress is inevitable while we live among both Noongar and wadjela people in a divided society?

Of course, I'd rather it were different.

I earlier quoted something from a letter written by Ethel Standley, my grandmother's cousin. She was angry when she realised that, because her father and uncle had taken Noongar women as their partners, they wouldn't be numbered among the pioneers. There's a strange mix of shame and pride in her reaction, I think. My grandmother's brother, Will Coleman, must have been proud to have been explaining Noongar place names by way of language and the associated stories. Something like pride enabled such relatively isolated individuals to retain something of language and its stories of place while they remained in their ancestors' country. Was it shame then, that kept them apart from other Noongars? Pragmatics and compromise?

It was pride made my father brag about his Noongar relations in Pa Tjinjel and Kayang Hazel's earshot, but also implicit in his boast was his ability to 'run with the hares and hunt with the hounds'. Of course, none of 'the hares' would've put it like that back then; it's an expression used by an early twentieth-century bureaucrat to express his frustration at the legislative limits of definition and control of Aboriginal people.

'He's our family,' Pa Tjinjel had said. 'Wait for him to ask.'

Maybe my father was too proud. After all, what was he doing bragging about Aboriginal relations, yet not knowing of — and not asking about — connections beyond the few he knew, who lived mostly among the white community? What did he mean, telling me as a child that 'Aboriginal people are better than the place they've been given,' that 'we are better than that'? Bearing in mind Kayang Hazel's comment about some fair-skinned Noongars in those years, it could be argued that my father was merely an arrogant man who thought he was better than everybody else. Maybe.

Perhaps these members of our extended family were trying to refuse the imperative to decide — an imperative created by colonisation — and were trying to be something else altogether.

One school of thought says that those families whose elders gained certificates — 'dog tags' — exempting them from repressive legislation applicable only to Aboriginal people, also gave away their entitlement to call themselves or their descendants Noongar. It's an argument that would equally exclude those who moved in white society without the humiliation of carrying 'dog tags'.

Kayang Hazel, although relatively fair-skinned, was the eldest in a family of predominantly dark brothers and sisters. She never had a dog tag.

Uncle Lomas laughs every time he tells a story about when he and his brothers Aubrey and Cedric had a puncture as they were driving between Borden and Gnowangerup. Humphrey Woods was with them too. A car pulled up to see if they needed help; Lomas and Aubrey were under the car trying to get it jacked up, and the relatively fair-skinned Cedric and Humphrey were beside the car. 'No, we're right,' said Uncle Cedric. 'We're just showing these *Aboriginals* how to change a wheel.'

Roberts men. Taken at Armadale, c. 1985.
Back row (left to right): Cedric Roberts Snr, Darryl Brown,
William Brown, Mal Brown. Middle row: Johnny Roberts
(Buddy), Aubrey Roberts Snr, Fred Tjinjel Roberts (Pa Tjinjel),
Lomas Roberts. Front row: Lenny Roberts, Aubrey Roberts.
(Photo courtesy of Elaine Miniter)

There's no doubt that Kayang Hazel and many of the family are bitter about those people — sometimes blood relations — who didn't want to know Noongars. Some people would cross the street rather than talk to you, she says. Her nephew Ed Brown says he used to be angry about that sort of thing too, until he learned how oppressive and restrictive the legislation had been: the 1905 Act and its amendments which were officially in force for almost half the twentieth century, and in fact functioned for longer, could be applied to virtually anyone of Aboriginal descent who mixed with Aboriginal people. That helped him understand their behaviour, but of course he still finds it difficult when such people want to return to community, often wanting to prove themselves in some way or other but without taking the time to re-build relationships.

I guess there were conflicting imperatives in a time when being Aboriginal — even 'of Aboriginal descent' — could make you subject to harsh legislation. Despite the rhetoric we adopt in retrospect, escaping oppression — finding something more like freedom — must have been at least as powerful a force as pride in being Noongar, especially when there were so many penalties attached to it.

'I didn't really get on with your father,' she said, and told me that he and her husband, Harry Brown, used to spend a lot of time together, and that the last time she'd seen Tommy Scott was when his car pulled up out the front of where she was living. He and Harry had been partying for days, and he'd come to drop off a suitcase of Harry's clothes, but when he saw Kayang Hazel come shouting towards him he dropped the suitcase on the ground, jumped in his car and took off. Anyone who knows Kayang would agree that was probably the wisest thing to do. Remembering it, she laughed and told me Harry and Tommy both 'knew Noongars' all right — they didn't keep themselves apart, weren't ashamed of their Aboriginal family. She repeated that they chased women and drank together. 'Matter of fact the grog killed them both,' she said.

My husband Harry was a good man, kind, a good-hearted person, but he was raised amongst, and with, white people. His father died, see, and his granny was white. She raised him. They were out-and-about people, you know, compared to us. More educated than what we were, but they never had the education that we had, Noongar way. I think we had the better education, because we lived by the beliefs and traditions and the rules of our old people.

I think — well, it used to be — that some people raised by white people, they believe differently. They think they're better than the rest of 'em, you know. I've always found those people look down on our people, 'cause our people were bush people. And the ones who looked down were the ones who mixed with the white people and the 'think-they're-classy' people.

You know, when I first went to mix with town people, I found it very difficult, because we were set in our ways. We never wore flash clothes, and we went barefoot all the time. And, I think our manners were different.

Those families did nothing for my husband, you know. I mean to say, what was a nine-year-old boy doing being raised by white people, when he had uncles and aunties?

He grew up in one area, and we grew up in another area. I never had very much to do with him until he was fourteen when he came home to Mum and Dad's. That's where I met him. In Albany.

When I first set eyes on him, oh 1932 ... Ah, he was a winyan one, he was. We hated one another.

After that ... well, he never had a good life. We got together in the forties, and he was working with Jim Bunjee. That's who started Harry on the drinking and running women. He taught him to be a womaniser. I got sick of that. It was better, for a while, when we got away from there and he got a more stable job. The railways was good, but then Harry hurt his back and he just pensioned himself off, really.

Our kids always helped. Eight of 'em we raised together: Elaine, James, Mildred, Henry, Eric, Elizabeth, Olive, Maurice; with my baby dying like I said. Sometimes we had to put 'em in the mission, at Roelands and sometimes Marribank. It was hard, you know, but that seemed the best we could do. I was sick for a time, too. Sometimes there was no school for them otherwise.

All the years my husband and myself were working, well people absolutely used us. When we first went away to live together, before we ever got married, we took care of his two sisters, and two brothers and two cousins. When his stepfather went into hospital we had to help look after his mother and all the other children. We just had to, because we were getting work, and we had the motor.

We used to help the people down there, get contract jobs, take the boys out, sort of police them to see they did their work and that, keep them off the drink, feed them ... When we got the money for the job, we'd pay them all their wages, and go on and get another job.

When their relations died they had no money. Well, we booked up the funeral expenses, and then worked and we paid it off. I reckon that between 1960 and 1972 we must've helped our people bury about half of them that died.

Me and Harry split up in 1971. He had taken to drink. And we used to have all sorts of people coming up to our place. The boys and I would come home — my husband wasn't working then — Eric helped until he was fourteen and Henry worked with me until he was nineteen. We used to go out, drive to work, come back at night and there used to be a mob of drunken people on the doorstep. We put padlocks and chains on the doors, and on the gates, but they still used to come in through the fence. And drink got so bad down there that I decided I was going to leave the district.

I got fed up living a life like that, so I came up here to live with my daughter when she got sick. My husband came to stay with me for a while, but then he got a state house at Albany. But you know, things became so bad that I just couldn't go back. I never used to drink, and he couldn't leave it alone.

I spent a lot of my life helping other people. I feel sorry for people. I think I wasted a lot of time that way, really.

They only needed us because we could do things for them, you know. I remember Harry getting up about three o'clock in the morning and taking children to hospital. And we'd take a month or two months' supply of food for our families, and have a big mob of other people turn up. 'You got any flour, any sugar, any tea?' Like that.

A lot of people pretended they were helpless, but they could've gone out and helped themselves.

*

Uncle Lomas wrote this for us about Harry Brown:

> *Well, this man Harry was a gift from God in those days. What he had done was go around and talk to all the farmers in the Borden area and line up work, whether it was root-picking, fencing, shearing, tractor driving, harvesting, truck driving ... everything that had to be done on a farm ... Harry would start off with a new mob of boys. Harry was so good and honest the farmers would all get together and buy him a car or a ute because they knew he was honest. Some of the farmers around Borden and Gnowangerup called him prime minister.*

Harry could move between white and black communities, and so was able to act as a sort of cultural broker. No doubt his fair skin made him more acceptable to the farmers.

Uncle Lomas was never in a position to organise things like Harry did, and his experience is perhaps more typical of what it has meant to be Aboriginal. Even when he was allowed to attend school, a lot of the time they just gave him a football and told him to stay outside the classroom. Fighting won him some respect from a racist society, and he toured with George Stewart's boxing troupe. At a fighting weight of around ten and a half stone — something like sixty-seven kilograms — he fought anyone, any size, and violence was not confined to the ring. His nephew Ed Brown says Uncle Lomas was the 'boss' of the tiny country town of Borden. It was his territory, says Ed, and he'd fight at the drop of a hat.

Uncle Lomas says the police used to wait for him outside the boundary of town on Fridays to see if he'd had a drink with the farmer after the week's work.

Uncle Lomas spent a lot of time in jail, and violence has been a significant part of his life. He's not really proud of it — except for the time spent in the boxing ring — but mostly he didn't have much in the way of options. Those country towns had citizens more than ready to use the weaponry of racism to bludgeon any proud Noongar, and the law supported them.

He said policemen used to arrest him just so he'd be out of the way and they could visit his wife.

Insecurity, uncertainty and doubt

My father taught me to fight when I was very young. He'd get down on his knees and show me how to shape up. I'd try to hit him, and he'd deliver soft-hand pokes and slaps whenever I dropped my guard. It was one of the things he went out of his way to do, one of the things he wanted to share.

Our boxing lessons dwindled away over a year or two, and I was disappointed and surprised at the apparent shift in my father's attitude. Over the years he increasingly discouraged fighting. 'There'll always be someone who can beat you,' he said. 'The winner is whoever can do the worst thing first.' Were these the harsh lessons he was learning as leading hand of a gang of Noongar road-workers? The one who was able to go into town to buy the drinks, but also had the responsibility of getting the men to work next day? Or was he just coming to understand the dead end of violence, the trap it creates in oppressed communities?

It was the 1960s. He would have been in his mid-to-late twenties, telling me that; a boy, it seems to me now. In many ways a lost man, for all his swagger and pride.

Unlike Uncle Lomas, he didn't have the dark skin that attracted trouble, and he could drink in hotels.

Uncle Lomas first touched alcohol in the 1960s when his boss took him into town to celebrate his new legal right to drink. The next day was the first time he didn't turn up to work. 'Drinking rights' was the name Noongars gave to citizenship, since that symbolised equality.

Grog and violence have given Uncle Lomas some good times, but problems too. He's not alone in that.

Kayang Hazel left for the city at the beginning of the 1970s partly because of trouble arising from alcohol, but more generally because of the accumulated stress of living in a community bearing the legacy of some of the things she's recounted in these pages, the racist oppression and accumulated injustice. She's frank about alcohol abuse, break-ins and violence, and the exploitation of perceived family obligations.

Kayang hasn't always lived among a community of her people. Sometimes it's best not to, and you're most useful from outside and away. But not if you stay there.

Taking my lead from Kayang Hazel's determination to confront difficult things about ancestors, I recognise that mine avoided being classified as Aboriginal by white society. So were they 'traitors'?

Maybe — but to extend the not always helpful analogy of warfare and violent resistance, it was hardly an equal battle. Forcing all our ancestors into the mould of failed warriors as some sort of warped adjunct of the Gallipoli myth doesn't do justice to them or the situation. Warriors die, and too often they die in restricted, frustrating circumstances in which their strength, their violence, has been turned against themselves and their loved ones.

According to Kayang Hazel, Pa Tjinjel said our family didn't believe in payback, not after what happened at Cocanarup. Her grandson Ryan Brown — who *is* a fighter — asked me to imagine how it felt, hunting a kangaroo with a spear and having a white man shoot it from further away and come galloping past on his horse. 'They musta just lay down their spears when the guns come out,' he said.

But Uncle Lomas and Kayang Hazel don't say their old people gave up. If they laid down their spears, they did so only to take up other strategies, try different tactics. Not always successfully.

Kayang's and my family lines had deviated over recent generations, trying different strategies. Given that, maybe I was too late to be answering the imperative to declare myself one or the other, Noongar or wadjela.

Lynette Russell in *A Little Bird Told Me* says:

> While I am careful not to describe myself as an Aboriginal person — to do so would trivialise the experiences of those people who have struggled and fought for their survival — I proudly embrace having Aboriginal heritage.

This important distinction is a tribute to her sensitivity, and I envy her apparent freedom from the need to decide and commit. She's quite correct: the collective struggle against racism and oppression is a major component of most people's Aboriginal identity. But does that mean our children will also need to experience it? Is oppression, other than the historical experience of it, the best way to develop community and an array of future possibilities?

A friend told me he used to love playing football because it gave him a chance to hit wadjelas. Another, articulating his sense of

Aboriginality, bitterly recounts walking to school in the rain as a school bus full of jeering classmates went racing past.

Their attitudes are very understandable: having been subject to racism and exclusion, you want to reply in kind.

I know people who mistakenly believe that being Noongar means, in effect, accepting the place they've been given at the bottom of society, and that 'being black' is 'not being white'. Even more unfortunate is the belief that the *real* Aboriginal people are the down and outs, the itinerants, the 'parkies'. In which case, to affirm one's Aboriginality is to perpetuate the characteristics expected of a member of an oppressed community, and a sense of self that carries, to paraphrase Noel Pearson's words, 'the human right to misery, incarceration and early death.'

I also worry that being told to be proud of your Indigenous identity, especially without an informed historical perspective and relying only on empirical evidence — the legacy of that history of oppression — can mean being trapped in a reactive loop. In wanting to affirm your identity, and wanting confirmation of it, you perpetuate too much of the way things are now, and an Indigenous identity can even come to mean *don't* achieve, *don't* succeed, because success is associated with a 'white' identity.

That stridently political imperative to declare yourself one or the other — Noongar or wadjela — asks firstly for commitment, and if the answer is Noongar, implies not only dialogue and engagement with other Noongars, but also their affirmation. Shrill self-assertion is not enough, and it's not necessarily a comfortable or clear-cut process.

Referring to her own sense of identity, Ms Russell remarks:

> ... *confusion comes from fearing other people's reactions, especially those of Aboriginal people ...*

I know something of that fear of rejection, having knocked on doors that remain closed because the Noongars inside see a wadjela at their front door. I could list a lot of examples. I reckon Lynette Russell doesn't want to be called an opportunist, a johnny-come-lately. She might be told she's jumping on the gravy train, crawling out of the woodwork, a born-again-blackfella, a nine-to-five black.

These are all terms that have appeared in my lifetime in response to changing legislation that means declaring your Aboriginality may mean gaining access to a range of 'positive discrimination' policies and even employment in the Indigenous bureaucracy. For many of us, such employment is a way of supporting other Indigenous people and working for social justice; it's also a way of affirming our identity and even of being an 'activist'.

Claiming an Indigenous identity can mean taking on the role of 'cultural broker' — even if you don't want it — and in that role, working either to maintain or increase the distance between Indigenous and non-Indigenous communities.

There's a lot to be said for maintaining such a gap, and for separation. Indigenous communities have had too much intervention and interference. Preserving a gap between these communities and the 'white' community can promote healing and help consolidate a heritage. On the other hand, such a gap ensures the continuing need for brokers, and the maintenance of their power. The rise of an Indigenous bureaucracy and its brokers has not necessarily meant a corresponding improvement in Indigenous living standards. Remember Kayang's remarks about her ancestor, Bobby Roberts?

> I hate the white man who put the gun in my grandfather's hands, so they could get control over Noongars, and gave him the chains, so he could chain them up.

And white people are still doing that today, like with ATSIC and their black bureaucracy.

She's a feisty woman all right, is Kayang Hazel. Keeps us all on our toes. There's always plenty we can argue about, plenty of tension and division. No wonder some of us worry about the reaction of others to the identity we claim. For instance, an Indigenous academic at a local university rang Kayang Hazel after he was enlisted to be the master of ceremonies at a function organised to congratulate me on a literary award I'd won. There'd been fresh controversy about the Indigenous identity of certain staff members at the university, and about other writers who'd described themselves as Noongar, and so, understandably, he wanted to verify who I was. He did the right thing by me, contacting an appropriate elder, but even that meant putting himself in the firing line because later, at the function, Kayang gathered a group of people around her and recounted their conversation. She finished with a theatrical gesture towards the academic and stage-whispered, 'So I told him, "Yes, Kim is Noongar, and not just since 1967 like you!"'

Kayang Hazel and others in the family — not only those with darker complexions — occasionally speak bitterly about the number of 'wadjela Noongars' in the Indigenous bureaucracy. It's a common sentiment, I think. I even read it in a national newspaper (*Weekend Australian*, 9–10 October 1999): 'All the bros are on the streets and all the white-skinned Aborigines have the jobs.'

Not surprisingly, similar issues came up at Native Title meetings Kayang Hazel and her brother and sister invited me to attend with them. Since Kayang seemed to file all her paperwork under her mattress or beneath furniture cushions I tried to be helpful in a clerical sort of way: I kept records, took notes, wrote letters, did a little research, that sort of thing.

There was a lot of rivalry, a lot of conflict. Kayang Hazel seemed to insult nearly everyone. She said people weren't Noongars at all, not from her country anyway. She said they only knew about reserves and missions, that they came from somewhere else, that they were white people who didn't know anything about Noongar tradition. Again and again she insisted: Native Title is about who was here before the white people came. It's about who still knows the special places, the language and all that.

'Some of those people never wanted to know us, and now they're the biggest blackfellas out. It's all about the money.'

She must've hurt people, speaking like this. Perhaps it was out of retaliation that some sought evidence that Kayang had a white father, and argued that, since her mother was not born in Noongar country, she had no right to a Noongar identity. They focused on her relatively fair skin, and not the fact that she was claimed and raised by Noongar elders, that her mother had been accepted into Noongar ways, and that after her first husband's death his brother took on the dead man's role so that they would all remain as Noongar family. They didn't consider her knowledge of community, of genealogy, of sites and history and language.

So even Native Title becomes just another way of dividing people, providing an opportunity to dispute one another's Indigenous identity while prioritising white law and racism.

Kayang Hazel shrugs and laughs at a lot of this sort of criticism and conflict, but it leads me to think of other people who, disconnected from their heritage and people, suffer 'identity confusion' and mental health problems.

Over the time Kayang Hazel and I worked on this manuscript she had in her care, among others, two schizophrenic adult grandchildren. Their schizophrenia was not directly related to identity issues, but there often is a correlation.

Discussion of Indigenous identity is not unusual in the case studies of the Royal Commission into Aboriginal Deaths in Custody, and one in particular describes a young man 'of Aboriginal descent' standing on one leg in front of a mirror with the other foot resting on his thigh. You know, that iconic one-legged stance — you've seen it on tea towels. The report also notes that the boy made a boomerang a day or two before taking his life.

I reckon he must have been wondering who he was, how to be himself; must've been trying on personas from the paucity of those available to him.

A schizophrenic acquaintance of mine rubbed charcoal into his skin before running from his house to a nearby vacant block and standing, naked and yelling, among the grass trees in the same posture as the boy in front of the mirror.

Perhaps some of these people could be described as 'white Australians of Aboriginal ancestry', a phrase used in a magazine article (*Weekend Australian*, 2–3 March 2003) which continued:

> *Lin has become a little obsessed herself — ravenous for more information about her Aboriginality. This month, she will set off for western NSW to walk where her grandmother and mother did, to talk to more of their friends, to hopefully uncover more secrets. 'This has opened my mind,' she says. 'I was ashamed to realise I didn't know a lot about Aboriginal culture and history. I need to go and find out.'*

Lin's reaction is perfectly understandable, if a little naive. Where should she go to find out more?

Well, if she is seeking guidance about how she might think of herself it might be wisest to avoid Australian literature; certainly some of its non-Indigenous examples. In David Foster's award-winning novel *In the New Country*, one character, upon discovering his Aboriginal ancestry, immediately files a land claim, starts drinking flagons of cheap wine all day long, and tears his house apart to feed the camp fire in his backyard. Such literature only offers Lin, or anyone like her, a recycling of stereotypical interpretations of Aboriginality and ridicule of any motivation for restoring links to Aboriginal ancestors and building upon an Aboriginal heritage.

Similarly, the Aboriginal character in Anson Cameron's novel *Tin Toys* replies to the comment, 'It's coolest to be Koori,' by saying, 'I'm a bit of a fraud as a black person. I mean if black's an experience ... I've never had it. If it's an upbringing ... I've never had that. If it's culture, well it's never been mine. All I ever had of being black was the hate ...'

Important questions are raised here, but *Tin Toys* denies the possibility of meaningful answers. For instance, when the Koori character's (white) father drives through an Aboriginal reserve telling his son, 'These are your people,' the son, staring blankly through the windscreen, tells his father not to stop the car.

Significantly, Foster's and Cameron's Aboriginal characters have no engagement with history, or with other Aboriginal people, cultural elders or land, but instead rely upon mainstream expressions of their identity. Take away the hate, Cameron's novel suggests, take away the oppression and the affirmative action, and there's nothing left upon which to base a distinct, Indigenous identity. It's only politics, they suggest, and they seem to be hoping we can forget it. Get over it.

Stan Grant — an Indigenous writer — poses similar questions to those put by Foster and Cameron:

*If Aborigines are poor, I'm not an Aborigine; if Aborigines are
coal black, I'm not an Aborigine; if Aborigines are the victims
of injustice and bigotry, I'm not an Aborigine ...'*

This author finds solace in being descended from a particular and distinctive region, and in his genealogical connections to other descendants of the countless generations who've inhabited the area. He refuses any individual claim to special programs designed to redress social injustice because, as Kayang Hazel would say, he's able to 'stand on his own two feet'. His sense of Indigenous identity is inclusive of achievement in so-called 'white' ways and at the same time reaches back through history to access a pre-colonial heritage.

Stan Grant provides very different answers to those given by Foster and Cameron. Still, he can't help worrying that his relative success and social mobility have distanced him from his people. It's a familiar dilemma, but the possible solution of ignoring his own Indigenous community and its imperatives isn't really an option, though it may appear so to writers like Anson Cameron.

Perhaps these differing options and responses help explain why many people argue that we need more Indigenous people writing for themselves, rather than being written about.

It's relatively easy to find 'identity confusion' in at least some Indigenous individuals, just as it's easy to find evidence of how Indigenous communities are disadvantaged relative to the rest of Australia. I could cite various statistics to do with health, mortality, employment, life expectancy, income and so on to prove that, but instead I'd like to consider some of the ways Aboriginality is linked to Australia's psyche and sense of itself because I think there are issues of identity confusion and mental health there, too.

Anna Haebich recognises this in *For Their Own Good*, a study of how legislation and the development of rural communities affected Noongar people, and identifies a 'process of group formation amongst the new settlers: Aborigines provided a measure against which they could set their modest achievements and were a group against whom the settlers could join together in opposition ...'

In *Dark Side of the Dream*, Bob Hodge and Vijay Mishra have argued that the earliest West Australian colonists — isolated, far from home and wanting to re-create the mother colony — kept Aboriginal people outside of the society they were trying to form because that helped draw the circle tighter and fuse disparate fragments of home into one entity. Like Haebich, Hodge and Mishra suggest Aboriginality has had a structural role in Australian society.

My local community newspaper demonstrated a very similar way of thinking when, only a few years ago, it celebrated nationhood by emblazoning 'Australia Day' diagonally across the front page. One side of the diagonal showed a windmill, a man in a stockman's hat, and a sheep; on the other there was a kangaroo, an emu, a grass tree ... and a naked man balancing on one leg.

The same intellectual schema is revealed in our currency; each coin has the Queen's head on one side, while the other shows an indigenous animal, with one exception — the face of an Aboriginal elder.

A book published in the middle of the twentieth century after its author's retirement as a long-serving Chief Protector of Aborigines in Western Australia also outlined a place for Aboriginal people. Neville's *Australia's Coloured Minority: its place in the community* explains how to breed out all visible signs of Aboriginality and cut individuals off from their people, their country and their heritage. The 'real Aborigines' would soon die out, and the others would be 'uplifted', assimilated, absorbed. That thesis offers *no* place for Aboriginal people in Australian society, only that they be removed.

It's as if there's some ailment in the psyche of the nation insisting upon a certain place for Aboriginal people, a certain relationship between Aboriginal and non-Aboriginal Australia. Or else! It's not one beneficial to Aboriginal people.

Native Title legislation threatened that relationship, and so perhaps it's no surprise that the phrase 'insecurity, uncertainty, doubt' was so often used. It supposedly referred to the difficulty Native Title created for planning and enacting development projects, particularly in mining, agriculture and tourism, but I think the *insecurity*, *uncertainty*, and *doubt* were about something far more important, some deeper constitutional disorder.

Kayang Hazel's nephew Ed Brown invited me to attend a Pastoralist and Graziers' conference; 2003 I think it was. The theme was Native Title. Ed attended in his role with the National Native Title Tribunal, and I think he may have wanted some companionship. One dear old fellow stood up and spoke about the good relationships he'd had with 'his natives' in the past, but now …

'It's like …' he paused, searching for an explanation. 'It's like when I was on the train down in Perth the other day, and everything was fine. Then some Aborigines got on. You could feel it,' he said, 'the atmosphere changed.'

Many heads in the conference room nodded. Pretty well everyone understood what he meant.

It's insecurity, uncertainty and doubt about the foundations of our nation. About who can and will belong. It's certainly insecurity about the relationship between Indigenous and non-Indigenous Australians, and between nation and land. It's insecurity, uncertainty and doubt about who 'we' are.

Anecdotes from the earliest days of the Swan River Colony, my home city, demonstrate that this insecurity has been around for a while. One diarist records two men wrestling a tree a little way from the track he was walking along. Red-faced, panting, they were trying to tear it from the ground, and when the diarist asked what was going on, they told him that they walked past this same spot every day, and every day the tree spooked them. Every day they mistook it for a native, one of the blacks, watching them, about to attack …

Remember Bobby Roberts and J S Roe looking down upon a dead body in the sand dunes? As the sand swirled around them, they understood how fear and mistrust had caused his death when all he had to do was ask; all he had to do was scratch the surface of the earth.

In *Burning Bush: A Fire History of Australia*, Stephen Pyne discusses a similar state of mind, emphasising the stereotypical 'bushman' as representative of the nation's identity, one forever tramping the 'outback of empire' and surviving on 'begged or pilfered' scraps of culture:

> *To see the bush disintegrating before their touch, however, compromised the character of the bushman and gave the pioneering experience a dark side — the anti-epic, which communicated a haunting sense of failure, scepticism, and insecurity; the … outback, a place in which those who persevered were punished and those who endured did so with stoic fatalism; the endless track to nowhere, in which comradeship dissolved into isolation, and society into mobs of industrial nomads; a history in which the noble bushman, the putative pioneer of cultivation, ended as a half-mad swagman on an endless walkabout of exile …*

It's enough to make you wonder at the popular appeal of 'Waltzing Matilda' as a national anthem — the mad, jolly swagman, of no fixed address, a suicidal thief.

Maybe I'm lingering in the past, and should know better; things are clearly different now. Fear and mistrust, all that control-freak stuff, are in the past, not in contemporary Australia. The desire for 'reconciliation' is strong today, and there's a growing recognition of the need for healing the rift between Aboriginal and non-Aboriginal Australia, and for soothing all that insecurity, uncertainty, doubt.

Advertisements beam Australia's Aboriginality to the world as part of national image and identity. Planes fly Aboriginal art through the sky, and the 2000 Olympics' ceremonial symbolism of a white child accepting the hand offered her by an Aboriginal elder surely means something. Yet the statistics about the health of Indigenous societies remain profoundly damning.

Undoubtedly, there's a growing appreciation of Indigenous heritage and culture; we live in times characterised by the fraud, hoax and appropriation of Indigenous cultural material. You could point to a litany of examples from the literary and visual arts: the theft of designs and images, all the various borrowings, the various desires and longings.

I read a newspaper headline: *Link as timeless as land they love.* What group of people do you think the article was about? 'I wanted to bring my kids up in the bush and give them the same special upbringing I had.'

It's what many Aboriginal people might also say in English, but it's not Aboriginal people speaking, it's pastoralists. They're understandable sentiments, but in the context of the duration of pre-colonial Indigenous presence, let alone that of our shared history — the land theft, dispossession, racist oppression, and the hysteria induced by Native Title — I hear the shrill calls of the desperately jolly swagman's descendants; insecure thieves, wanting to really belong, yet only beginning to understand what that might mean.

The Yamatji artist Terry Shiosaki pointed that newspaper article out to me when we were working together in the inaugural year of an Indigenous arts course. Our students were Aboriginal people from all over Australia, though most were Noongars; some not long out of school, others mature and established in their community. Many of them, disconnected from their own people's traditional design, liked to do 'dot paintings' and felt compelled to provide a story to accompany their canvases and thus legitimise themselves as 'authentic' artists. There were clichés: red, black and gold maps of Australia, didgeridoos, boomerangs, kangaroos and tribal men silhouetted in that well-known stance; images drawn from political battles and tourist kitsch.

It was a rare forum to reflect on history and identity, authenticity and image, and one of our objectives was to discourage students from using the traditional designs and techniques of other Indigenous groups. Many students were also confronting for the first time the injustice of our shared history, their dispossession and the degree of their disconnection from the culture of their ancestors. Not surprisingly, in their desire to express their Aboriginality, many copied what was readily accessible in mainstream media as 'real' Aboriginal art, and thus participated in the reduction of the possibilities of Indigenous expression, and its simplification.

The alternative is an intimidating challenge: to search and reclaim cultural expressions from our own Indigenous ancestors, our own country; to devise expressions of spirituality from within ourselves, with whatever means at our disposal and arising from our histories. Personally, I don't think anything need be rejected simply because it came from non-Indigenous sources. Think of Kayang's memory of message sticks arriving in stamped envelopes, and what it suggests about communicating from the very heart of place while utilising new means to do so.

Anyway, I'm not engaged in the visual arts. I'm a writer, even if from the niche — that sub-category — labelled 'Indigenous writing'. I'm proud to be crammed among writers who range from those living in communities which retain their language and are embedded in traditional country, to those ground down by generations of racist oppression, and even those like myself: relatively disconnected, dispossessed and assimilated.

Actually, 'Indigenous writing' may not even be a sub-category of Australian literature, and I don't say that because many of its practitioners are working with narratives and forms which predate Australian literature. No, I say it because I have looked in bookshops for my own books and, failing to find them in the Australian Literature section, finally located them under 'Australiana'. Maybe that says something about the way major book chains are run, or perhaps it's further proof of that structural opposition and failure of inclusion which characterise Australia. As much as I didn't like being put in Australiana rather than Australian Literature, it's hardly unusual for a Noongar to deserve better than the place he's been allocated. Consider this one, for instance, caught in a pastoralist's snare of words:

> Freddie, who never demeaned himself by work of any kind, was something of a labour agitator and on one occasion I looked him up at the native camp … (I) found him sprawled on his back reading the Bulletin, with spectacles on his bitten off nose. This attitude together with his ape-like face and limbs, gave a general effect which was truly comic.
>
> (Dempster, cited in Rintoul)

It's a quote I know well and to which, perhaps perversely, I continually return because it seems so exemplary, so typical in many ways. There's the derogatory representation, the attempt at a pact between writer and reader, the absence of an Indigenous perspective, and the stunning arrogance.

In fact Mr Fred McGill was himself a writer, and in a letter to the *Kalgoorlie Miner* in 1897 complained of the treatment his people received. Although sometimes ambushed by the language, his appeals ring true:

> *The blackfellas were somewhat wild … They were wild because of white men shooting into their camps …*
>
> *I have attended to the sick and dying Aborigines and spent all my hard earning among them and what with the very little aid obtained from the West Australian Government, my burden has been a very heavy one.*
>
> *I write to know why we cannot obtain some of that 5000 pounds voted by the West Australian Government for our support …*
>
> *Some white people as a rule are very good … but on the other hand, should I send any native brethren to buy goods — bread in particular — some of the business men hold the article in one hand while the other is held out for money and, in nine cases out of 10, no change is given …*

Fred McGill and Bobby Roberts were countrymen and had a lot in common. Fred had guided an expedition led by Forrest — later Western Australia's first premier — along the south-east coast of Western Australia in 1870. He also helped establish at least one pastoral lease. A talented and generous man, he learned to read and write, but by the time he was writing to the newspaper his home society had been damaged and diminished by colonisation. Just imagine what he and Bobby Roberts might have achieved — and been able to contribute — in more just circumstances.

No wonder 'Freddie' made the pastoralist feel insecure; no wonder he was kept to the 'native camp'. Attempting to reduce land-theft and invasion to an issue of industrial relations, the pastoralist calls him a 'labour agitator'. Fred McGill's very presence must have made the family consider, perhaps even doubt, the morality of their enterprise.

My ancestral countryman would have read 'Australia for the white man' on the *Bulletin*'s masthead and felt unwelcome and excluded. It's no surprise that many Indigenous writers advocate doing something similar in return — 'exclude them back' — show them how it feels.

It's a powerful argument championed by, among others, the man best known as Mudrooroo. Mudrooroo began life as Colin Johnson, and although arguably not a Noongar — and we do argue about these things — he apparently grew up among Noongars, and knew the racism and hostility of Western Australian country towns. He was prepared not only to speak on behalf of Aboriginal people everywhere, but also to be very prescriptive and draw lines of exclusion and inclusion. His book *Writing from the Fringe* advocated marginalising white readers, and Johnson was also fulsome in his praise of the Murri poet Lionel Fogarty who, in the foreword to his *New and Selected Poems*, says:

> I know how white Australians write and I know how they
> talk. They'll never come near the fourth world. White man
> will never know.

It's a very understandable attitude. Given what we know of colonial history, of the cultural damage and racism inflicted upon Indigenous people, it makes sense. It also promotes solidarity in one's own community, using a method similar to that employed, some say, by the white community: exclusion and opposition.

But if that's all we do, it's not enough. Undoubtedly my life experience is different from Lionel Fogarty's, and perhaps that's why I'm averse to intentionally writing that way. I certainly don't think it's what literature does best.

Of course, plenty of people would disagree with me. In fact, many aren't all that interested in literature. I remember a friend coming up to me at a function and saying as he shook my hand, 'Deadly. They like that literary thing, unna?' I think he considered literature as some sort of confidence trick, and — since he'd consider himself as an activist — only useful as a strategic means of achieving some tangible end.

Someone who'd asked me to write a book with them did so with the proviso: 'Don't make it like that other one [*Benang*] that Noongars can't read.' I winced at that, but had to laugh too.

At a school meeting to choose prizes for our children, I heard a parent saying: 'Don't give them books. Noongars don't read books!'

Well, I do read books, and I write them; and writing this one with Kayang Hazel continually forced me to confront my own peculiar, anomalous 'place in the community' — the apparently flimsy basis of my Indigenous identity, and to question the role of an Indigenous writer.

Of course there are problems for any Indigenous writer, not least the fact that those with whom you most identify form a minority of your readers.

So what do you do?

Hand over 'cultural understandings' to enlighten a mainstream audience?

Marginalise that audience; show them how it feels?

What about generating slogans with which your few Noongar

readers might agree, repeating — especially — the sort of things they'd like said to wadjelas?

Perhaps you should write of a people's oppression so that the majority of your readers might vicariously experience it.

I think we can do all these things, and hopefully more.

Eduardo Galeano, in his 'In Defence of the Word', suggests:

> *In saying: 'This is who I am,' in revealing oneself, the writer can help others to become aware of who they are.*

When I was asked to give a public lecture on race, identity and history, I asked Kayang Hazel what she thought needed to be said, and what sort of things I should say.

'Let people know you're Noongar,' she said. 'Be proud of yourself, we're all proud of you. You just be you, Kimmy.'

She might be feisty, but she's not prescriptive. Her answer sprang from something like faith, and her encouragement and trust came from an old belief that each of us is one among many possible manifestations of the place we live in, and that recognising shared descent from specific country can be more powerful than sharing oppression. In Kayang Hazel's answer I recognise the Noongar ways of Mokare, of Yagan, and even the early Bobby Roberts.

Wilomin Noongar, Kayang Hazel said, and I thought of those of us who are not recognisably Aboriginal. Disconnected, dispossessed, we become visible only when our eyes are opened to history. Acknowledging our people — wanting recognition and welcome — we call out. The wilo call is also associated with death, with the spirits of Noongars not so far from Cocanarup.

Wadjela Noongar. I was lured by the sound of Noongar voices, and the demonstration of how certain stories of kinship and regeneration are so deep in the land, but I also want to acknowledge and celebrate my non-Indigenous family and, by extension, all aspects of Australia's heritage. I don't see how that can be justly done without the primacy of Indigenous culture and society being properly established.

I live in Noongar country, have Noongar ancestors and extended Noongar family. It was Noongar people who created society here, and their reactions to 'first contact' — as described in earlier chapters of this book — offer mostly sound values upon which to build, and within which 'white' society could be accommodated. Unfortunately our shared history has demonstrated that the alternative — accommodating Noongar society within 'white' society — has proved impossible, to the detriment of what we all might be. As I see it, this is reason enough to offer those who insist on asking why a small amount of Noongar blood can make you a Noongar, while any amount of white blood needn't make you white. It's a considered public position, intended to foreground inequalities in our society, and particularly in our history.

Of course, I don't know what it's like to be part of a traditional Indigenous community but, as Ambrose Mungala Chalarimeri in *The Man from the Sunrise Side* says of his old people: 'They are gone but I am still here.' There's a weight of responsibility in that phrase.

Some of us, variously estranged from our Indigenous heritage, want to respectfully consolidate that past in ways that generate momentum into a positive future. That's a continuing struggle, and about more than survival:

> *Our collective identity is born out of the past and is nourished by it — our feet tread where others trod before us … but this identity is not frozen into nostalgia. We are not, to be sure, going to discover our hidden countenance in*

> *the artificial perpetuation of customs, clothing, and curios*
> *which tourists demand of conquered peoples. We are what*
> *we do, especially what we do to change what we are: our*
> *identity resides in action and in struggle …*
>
> (Galeano, 'In Defence of the Word')

Action and struggle don't mean only overt politics, or battles. Writing — this making of small marks upon a page which is sometimes like beginning a journey, even a collective journey, a gradual one-at-a-time bringing together of hearts and minds as a way to contribute to a Noongar and increasingly wider, sense of community — is also action and struggle. As is continuing a heritage from before colonisation and, grafting and growing, shaping something new from those roots.

My father's experience was different from that of Kayang Hazel and her siblings, just as my own is from many of those in the Noongar community. I think Indigenous experience can encompass both pride and shame, and can even include complicity in processes of colonisation.

In writing this, in talking about such things, Kayang Hazel and I — along with others descended from the same people — looked searchingly across the generations, trying to understand what had happened, feeling for what we have in common and where we differ, who we are and what we might be.

Increasingly Kayang talked about her childhood and, accompanying her on those reminiscences, I heard stories that seemed less rehearsed; fragments of what she herself had heard as a child.

Dingo Country

We used to take the sheep out, and we had to make sure we shut the gate. There was box leaf poison. There was a dingo too, and he was doing a lot of killing.

Aunty Evelyn was staying with us, and Uncle Stanley.

We could hear all the sheep bleating. Daddy said to go early and bring in the ewes and lambs and that. It was about three o'clock.

So we go out fetching sheep. We had a little rifle, one of those little garden guns, you know. We knew how to use it, it was our protector.

Aunty Maggie was the eldest, she was about eleven, I was about nine, and Lenny was seven. She didn't know how to shoot a gun, you know; she wouldn't know how to pull the trigger. But we were well and truly learned; we knew about guns, and we had to be careful with a gun, you know, Dad used to show us what a gun could do if it was mishandled and if you never used a gun properly it could kill you, or harm you.

Anyway, as we were going, Daddy said, 'Take the gun just in case you see the dingo.' Anyway, we went through the paddock there, and we were coming towards the hill there, and we followed the sheep pad through all this wilyaworri grass, shepherd's bush. Sheep pad go right in the middle see, and it goes straight down and then over the rise and then down in the hollow.

Well, when we got on this hill, we looked over there, and we could see the sheep all moving, see, sheep all moving. They were running. They must've smelled the dingo, but the dingo wasn't worrying about the sheep. I think he must've been worrying about his bitch see, his bitch musta been on heat or something. He was smelling her, coming for her.

We could see all these sheep, and the sheep must've smelled the dingo 'cause they were all moving pretty fast. And as we were going down this bird started to talk.

Well, when magpies start talking — magpies, like they're stickybeaks — they'll tell you when things and people are around.

'Hey,' I said, 'something must be here.' You know, 'cause they'll tell you. They act as a signal. Like if human beings come, or anything that they know, they'll talk. These magpies, I don't think they were warning us, they were warning this other person, that we were predators or whatever.

I said to Lenny, 'Give me the gun.'

'No,' he said, 'you can't shoot. Girls can't shoot, only boys can shoot.'

And he had the gun ready, see. He had his hand on the trigger, and he's walking. And he walked around this big rock, and when he turned this side, he come face to face with the dingo.

Well, the dingo's there. And Lenny's there with the gun. I'm behind him, and Aunty Maggie further behind.

The dingo stood and looked at him. He could've hit it right there. Could've had a try.

He shouted, and he put the gun up in the air, and he pulled the trigger.

Bang!

That big red dog just took off.

Lenny was shaking like a leaf, and the tears were running out of his eyes. And I was cruel wild.

Lenny said, 'Don't you tell Daddy about this. Don't you tell him about this.'

I was that wild, true. Anyways, we rounded the sheep up, and brought them through the gate, put them in the yard.

We lit a big fire.

Daddy wasn't home. He used to go one way on the horse checking the traps, Mummy used to go the other side, checking that way, see. She took the dogs with her. No dogs at home to bark. They were away all night, see.

Grandfather had his *kornt* — hut — over that side. He went to sleep.

In the night I thought I saw sheep jumping see, sheep jumping like this. Away from us. Couldn't see 'em properly.

Next morning, went to let the sheep out. There were two, three sheep there with teats eaten. Sheep bleeding. Sheep there dead, dingo slaughtered a lot of sheep and he never ate one! Just ripped them apart, mutilated them and took off.

Well. Daddy said, 'Just fancy that dingo's got so brave.'

'Yeah,' Aunty Maggie said, 'wasn't for Lenny,' she said. 'If Lenny would've give the gun to Hazel she would've shot it. He wouldn't shoot it,' she said. 'He just put the gun up in the air and pulled the trigger and dingo went.'

So Pa went looking around for where this dingo went, like places it might go for water. Found its tracks. Dingo track is bigger than a fox track, and he never puts his claws out. Like a cat at toilet. And Pa found the place where it went, a freshwater creek. There's a rock there, and he used to come from the bank and jump onto the rock, and then put his foot down and drink the water.

So Daddy went and shot a parrot, *karwa*, and opened it up and put poison inside it. Thinking he gunna catch it like that. So, he put the parrot there.

But dingo didn't want the parrot. He just wanted to go and have his drink see.

Daddy looked where the dingo jumped, and he set the trap there, see?

Old man never used to use brown paper, because brown paper too hard. Won't break. He used to use *Western Mail*, 'cause paper was thin. Just enough to cover the mouth of the trap, stop the sand from getting in.

That night we heard a dingo howling. Get up and grab the gun. Dingo in the trap.

That dingo been caught before. One front paw only had two toes on the end.

He caught forty-eight dingoes in a trap in two weeks. All sorts of dingoes. Black and tan, creamy ones, red ones. Lot of dingoes.

Dingo country, that's Jerramungup, Needilup, Quaalup, Cape Riche, Bremer, Dillon Bay.

They used to go all night for traps, Daddy and Mummy.

Used to be nothing for us, you know, going toilet, going in the bush or even going for a walk, or going hunting and that, to see two or three dingoes running along in front of you.

They used to come and drink outta the same dam that we used to go and get washing water from. We used to get out drinking water from the tank at the shed, down at the house.

Always see their tracks around the dam.

We had a dog, big dog, he wouldn't kill a dingo. He'd fight 'em and bite 'em, but he wouldn't kill 'em.

Dingoes will howl out and call each other until they come together. When we lived out in the bush in the early thirties, that was a normal sound.

Fox makes that little *warra* sound, little shivery sound.

Saw a pitiful sight, once. We were coming back from Doubtful Island. Boys were catching salmon down there. We caught two groper, we caught some skippy. Got a lot of shellfish and crabs too. We were coming through the peppermints. It was all sand, coming out to where the road joins the Quaalup road.

Come to a sandy patch, right around the corner, and there's this dingo standing in the middle of the road, and he's got a full salmon in his mouth. You could count every bone in that poor dingo's body. I reckon he must've been about fifty or sixty years old. He was blind, and he must've been deaf. And he was standing right in the middle of the road.

Winyan. Poor fella.

I said, 'Kill him. Put him out of his misery.'

Daddy said, 'The salmon's gunna kill 'im, let 'im eat it.'

Salmon poison you when the sun's been on it, see.

One time, this was years later, we found a print, a dingo footprint on a rock. This was at the mouth of the river. Me and Audrey and Ray. Ray was her de facto. There was a round rock with dog imprints on it. True Kimmy, true as God.

I'd like to show you that rock too. Just like where a dog was standing, it was. Two prints, back foots.

Musta been a story for that, like where the dogs run into the sea at that other place.

I said to Ray, 'Don't take that rock.' But Ray picked up the rock and put it in the back of his four-wheel drive.

He took the rock back to Audrey's place in Gnowangerup, and the rock's still there now for all I know. But a couple of nights later — nobody had touched it, nobody had washed it — the footprints were faded.

They're not there any more. True, they were jet black, Kimmy. Jet black like that. Dog's feet, clear as you like.

My Tex said, 'Ray, you mustn't touch that. That belongs to old Noongars, you mustn't take it.' But he didn't listen.

Rock was there, and Ray took the rock, and now it's got no footprints on it. Yeah, big smooth one.

Dingoes, wild dogs, they're very important animals to us. You've read Mrs Hassell's book, unna? Old Noongar, he wore dingo tails. But they only told her what they wanted her to know. Sometimes he ate puppies, the Noongar, and dingo'd chase 'im, dig up the trees if he climbed up 'em. So they say. Lotta stories like that.

See, there's places people don't know about. I'll take you and show you. Like the place where the dogs jumped into the sea. They were hunting, old Noongar and his dogs. He had a lotta dogs, his own and his brother's dogs with him too. His brother went away, see, so he had too many dogs really, too many dogs. Made it hard to hunt 'cause it's hard to control 'em. They take off all at once, excited, just rip into kangaroo, emu, whatever it was, see.

You know Sealin Garlett, unna? His kangaroo dogs, they deadly boy. They won't chase a kangaroo till he tells them. He makes one dog stay, the other chase the roo. Cleverest dogs ever. He got 'em that well trained. But this old Noongar down that way …

Like, his dogs chase after an emu. All the dogs took off after one emu. Ate it up. When the man got there, nothing left for him. Just the feet, feathers, you know.

They saw a young kangaroo, a doe. Same thing. Dogs chased it, got it, ate it all up. Same thing. Nothing left for the old Noongar when he got there, only the feet and skin and that.

The dogs kept fighting, ripping into it, and eating all the meat up, see. They only left rubbish for him.

He left. Just walked away, and the dogs followed him. He travelled down the coast way, walking through the dunes. Lots of little kangaroos, *damar*, like quokkas at Rottnest Island.

Dogs happy, hunting. Plenty of food for them, but same thing. Nothing left for the Noongar. And he couldn't hunt for himself 'cause so many dogs, scaring everything away.

'Oh well.' He just lay down. Found himself a nice spot in the shade, lay down. Mmmmm … kept his eye on the dogs but.

Bit later, he lit a little fire and lay down next to it. He kept his eye on those dogs. Wave a stick at them, chase 'em away, if they come too close.

He's nice and warm by his fire. Pretending that he's

sleeping, except if they come close. Keeping one eye open, all the time.

They fall asleep. The dogs fall asleep, and he was waiting for them to do that, because when they did he grabbed a stick from the fire — karlmaat they say — and he snuck away.

You know what he did, unna?

Bit later, those dogs wake up, and the wind! That wind was screaming, boy. And hot! A circle of fire all around them, 'cause that Noongar made a fire all around them, except for near this cliff, see, and the wind blowing that way.

They're all running and howling, and they couldn't get away. They had to jump. They jumped, they jumped for the water.

Smoke, and fire everywhere. They jumped and they fell and they slid. Swam out into the sea.

They turned into seals. Their legs were burned off. The Noongar, he climbed up high, to look out you know. Smoke everywhere. And he turned into a stone. It's still there, like a memorial, you know. Like a monument. And you could still see it, I remember seeing it. You could see where all the dogs slid down too.

Not so far from Ravensthorpe.

They reckon those dogs kept swimming. They kept swimming, all the way to down near Jerdacuttup somewhere. I dunno, maybe near where Granny Winnery musta camped, where they came from, those people, just to get killed that time.

Popped their heads up.

Dwoort baal kaat — *dog his head.*

That's how you say seal, unna? Head like a dog. Seals are supposed to be related to dogs.

You ever hear them singing out? Like barking.

When you look at a seal, their eyes are similar to a dog. But they got no feet, and they got flippers.

*

Dwoort baal kaat.

There had been only mute stone; now wild dogs howled and leapt into the sea through flames, were transformed into seals.

We walked along the beach sand and rocks. A seal reared its head from the sea, looked at us with what seemed keen interest …

I grew up in Albany, hundreds of kilometres away to the west of the place where this story resides, and almost every day went past a huge stone known as Dog Rock. It's the shape of a dog's head — or seal's — and its collar of black and white paint and the curve of the road to detour around it shows what a traffic hazard it is. In fact, I only ever knew it as part of a narrative of road safety, or the tourist kitsch of postcards, yet an old story might make something quite different of it; have it shaking off bitumen and black and white collars, and leaping from postcards.

I don't know that particular story, but I know how special it is to visit stone and earth formations and hear the stories and words intrinsic to them. I know how it feels to become one among a people uttering those sounds, re-telling those stories. I say 'become' rather than 'be' because, for me at least, it's about recovery, in both senses of the word: reclaiming a heritage, and restoring health.

Stumbling, mumbling sounds of an old language, searching for the footprints of its spirit. Perhaps these are feeble gestures in a land of winter-green crops, summer-razed stubble, of ribbons of bitumen and leaning fence-posts and rising salt, whose life-forms — the many possibilities of its spirit — are variously dispersed, or huddle together, hesitant.

Kayang Hazel, her brother and sister and their children led me to various places in their traditional country, a thin strip of coast whose rivers wend their way across plains of sand and mallee, between granite domes, and barely reach the sea.

Some say these rivers are tired, have failed, and express only futility. But there are other ways of understanding them.

Some Wilomin Noongar elders, c. 2007 (left to right):
Helen Hall (nee Nelly), Lomas Roberts,
Gerald Williams, Hazel Brown, Audrey Brown.
(Photo courtesy of Wirlomin Noongar Language and Stories Project)

Default Country

A lexical cartographer and researcher for the Australian National Dictionary, Jay Arthur, has suggested that English-speaking Australians are trapped in 'the Default Country' because, although living in one geographical place, our language originates in another. It's not exactly that the 'land of the English language' is England, but rather that 'our language is set to the Default Country'. Arthur continues:

> The Default Country ... is narrow, green, hilly and wet, which makes Australia wide, brown, flat and dry. In the Default Country the rivers run all the year round ... They know how to find the sea.

The word 'drought' in a country where rainfall is naturally irregular, says Arthur, encourages us to be disappointed, to feel cheated, to see the land as hostile.

And the word 'river' only approximates what in Australia is known as a river. Along the south coast a 'river' is typically a tenuously linked sequence of ponds barred by a sandy beach from reaching the sea.

Perhaps the English language — yes, even 'Australian English' — carries ways of thinking which correspond awkwardly with the country we inhabit.

We need a rethink.

Kayang Hazel tells me the Noongar word for river is *bily*. It's also the word for navel.

Think of those south coast rivers as connection to a nurturing life source; as patience, as stillness and welling. Water seeps from springs, from soaks, from natural wells, and accumulates, ebbs and flows, only occasionally gathering sufficient momentum to break through the sand, tossing it aside as it rushes to the sea.

We were at a roadhouse, beside a petrol bowser. Across the road a dry, grass-stubbled paddock sloped to a relatively close horizon. I was asking Uncle Lomas about a story in the Hassell memoir, *My Dusky Friends*, in which the moon and a kangaroo talk about what will happen when they die. I'd interpreted it as an archetypal mortality story. Uncle Lomas gave me his version. Yes, he said, the kangaroo's bones will dry and crack in the sun, will become grey and shine silver in moonlight, until the hill grows up around them. But although the moon also dies, it is continually reborn. He told much of the story in Noongar language, which I struggled to understand, and he seemed to suggest that we are part of a continual rebirth because we carry the shape of the new moon at the base of our fingernails. I remember looking at his dark hands, the half-moon bright in his thumbnail. It doesn't shine so brightly in my own.

He pointed across the yellowing paddock. 'That story comes from over there.' Later, we walked to a rock-strewn dome in the middle of a cleared, dusty paddock and I saw the sequence of waning circles in stone.

This is country where the remaining pockets of bush are remarkable for their biodiversity, and the larger areas — like Fitzgerald River National Park — are internationally recognised for their uniquely resourceful and resilient flora.

That same afternoon we went to a place popularly known as Nightwell. I'd heard about it, read about it also in *My Dusky Friends*. Some maps give it the Noongar name Kiapanwymburup. During the day it was a dry, rocky crevice, but at night fresh water rose plentiful and sparkling within it, only to disappear again with the dawn.

It was dynamited in the late nineteenth century in an effort to make it a more permanent water source, and destroyed.

We got there late in the day. The sky was overcast and bruised, and gravel crunched under our feet as we walked away from the car until our footsteps became muffled and the trees whispered above our heads.

'Nidja kwel maya wangin,' I said. *The sheoaks are talking.*

Uncle Lomas looked at me. I think he was surprised.

I said it again. He corrected my pronunciation of one word, and said, 'Old Noongar, he'd understand what you're saying.'

All that remains of Nightwell is a small pool, a puddle. Algae hung in its water, tadpoles flicked here and there, and broken rocks were scattered around it. Uncle Lomas told me the name he knew it by, and made me repeat it several times until I got it right.

I told him I'd read how a surveyor set explosions to try and make Nightwell a permanent water source and destroyed it.

'Yeah,' he said, 'but they reckon it's starting to work again. Come here night-time, and there's good water like it just a bit further up.'

Kayang Hazel didn't always share his optimism.

You know, when they take away trees and plants, and they interfere with wildlife, all those things are lost.

Every time we go to Quaalup, through Ravensthorpe, through Jerramungup, you see the sand banking up against the fences. Some parts of the fences along the Albany Highway are only about so high above the sand.

Sand. Sand blowing and blowing. There's nothing. Nothing stable to hold the sand. And when that north wind is blowing, you get your dust storms, and you get blinded. They reckon God said that man is gunna destroy the world.

I see an old Noongar man years ago. He was sitting down rubbing on a *wana* stick. He never do it with a spear, always grab some poor old woman's wana stick and sitting down rubbing it, rubbing it with his sticks. And then a thunderstorm come ...

My brother Stanley was there, he saw that too. I reckon he would've wanted to bring the rain like that himself, put out the fires they set to clear the bush. See, he used to help do the clearing, lighting fires and that. He couldn't choose. You didn't have a choice most of the time.

He used to come back on weekends and he used to be very moody and upset. And he used to drink a lot. He said, 'I wish I could get another effin' job. I don't like what I'm doing.'

I said, 'Why don't you like your job?' He was driving the bulldozer, see.

'You know what?' he said. 'I'm driving this effing machine over the ground I know we walked on. And girl, you should see it now. If you go back there ... Those trees where we used to sit under, where Mummy used to be pegging the skins out ... the old camp,' he said, 'we went right over that.'

'And when the fire goes through,' he said, 'there might be nothing left to show anybody that our people ever been there.'

About five months after that it was February. The fire season opened on the fifteenth of February, and the seventeenth of February we were coming back from Bremer and they were lighting the fires to do the burn-off. This fire was burning twenty-eight miles wide. They were doing the burn-off, and the fire got away from them, see. And it was a north wind.

It would have cleared every farm in the district, but for the sea breeze coming in. And these Noongars got on this side, and they burned the fire with the sea breeze and the wind took it back.

But the smoke! You couldn't see!

We stopped at Boxwood Hill and this fire was raging. Aunty Edna was with me, and Joseph Woods was driving the motor. I said, 'You see that smoke?' We couldn't see the blaze. I said, 'You see that black smoke rolling? That smoke's sending everything that we hold dear up there to the sky. It's gunna rain down on us.'

Only landmarks now is, well, when you're leaving Jerramungup and you're going towards Bremer, the first creek there. Tjaanak Creek. Devil's Creek. That's the untouched place. But apart from that, all razed, and farms right through.

Me and old boy, Johnny's father — Lenny — he came down there to help us when we was working. There were three *ngaw* nests in this moort clump. And he cleared all around it. One nest was back here, and the two down the bottom like that.

'Hey sister,' he said. 'You come here.'

And there's this big white ant nest, like big *worting*. He said,

'You remember this place?' And he looked at me, and his eyes were full of tears.

I said, 'Yes,' I said, 'I remember this place. I remember this place.'

That was a special place where we used to go and get eggs. Where Jerramungup townsite is now, where they ploughed over on this side now, there was seven ngaw nests, in just that little area.

You know, when we lived out there, you could go to any creek out there at all. You didn't have to carry buckets full of water, or drums of water like you have to do now when you're travelling. You could go to any creek and find fresh water running. And now, since they did the clearing, you can see salt, you can see trees dead everywhere. All around the creeks that used to be fresh water, they're all salt water now.

I hate people cutting down trees. I was a contractor myself. For every mallee root I chucked on a heap and burned, I really needed the tree to still be growing on top of it. Every log that I burned, I needed alive.

I hated doing that job, but I had to make a living, you know.

What white people did, see, they changed the Noongar people's lifestyles. They changed Noongar people. White man helped to make Noongars greedy. That's the way I look at it. They not only changed our country Kim, they changed our people too.

When we first went to Borden to live, it was scrub. Now there's hardly any trees in the district. All finished now.

Farmers, they're plagued with salt. They got sand up against their fences. And who to blame but themselves?

It's funny. Laughable really. You go down there and you see

people growing trees. You say, 'What they growing those trees for?' For sheep shade! And yet, when they cleared the land they knocked down every bush and every tree. Weren't they thinking about the animals that they were gunna raise? Put a big shed on top of them.

When they did that land development, they never stopped to think. They wanted every inch cleared, to put a piece of grain, a bit of seed or something. To grow a crop. They never thought about the trees. Taking all the trees away, that encouraged the salt to come up and claim the land. They haven't got very much farm land there; and the salt has got it all.

Very badly planned.

Noongar, years ago, when they used to burn bush, they used to select the areas that they used to burn. They selected the areas. And they lit one fire. They didn't have fires all over the place.

They were very careful.

*

Something — it might be progress, or it might be the need for short-term profit — has caused a lot of damage to country on the south coast. Government had a slogan to inspire land clearing — *a million acres a year* — and the earth was injected and laced with chemicals.

Maybe individual farmers can't be held responsible: it was a time of 'land settlement' initiatives, with government policies promulgating such attitudes, encouraging such thinking. As the 2003 documentary, *A Million Acres a Year*, makes poignantly clear, farmers were damaged as well.

Despite all this, many older Noongars are nostalgic about shearing and working on farms. Much of Kayang Hazel's working life was spent as a rural labourer of one sort or another, and it was the same for most of her siblings and many of their children. Her relationship with the land includes working it in a 'white' way, along with the friendships, memories, and respect she gained from doing so. The same applies to Uncle Lomas. When his car broke down out in the country he walked to a farm where he'd once worked and asked to use their telephone to get help. The farmer insisted Uncle Lomas borrow his Mercedes.

Driving through the country with Kayang Hazel and her siblings is to hear yarns triggered not only by geographical features and Noongar place-names, but also by signposts, even by individual trees and fences. The geography and place names unfold into creation stories, but there's a fascinating social history triggered by the more ephemeral markers as well. That old fence was made by Uncle Lenny, its jam tree (mangart) posts grey with age; here's where we camped, shearing, and the boys killed rabbits with their *dowak*. This was where a car overturned, or where someone died, or saw a spirit hitch-hiking. See that paddock? Uncle Lomas was the first to drive a brand new harvester there. No-one else — white or black — had any experience, but he'd driven one like it on a farm a couple of days drive away.

Uncle Lomas liked to call in on farmers as we drove back from our visits to country. We'd have a cup of tea; they'd offer to fuel up our car.

Like Kayang Hazel, he's proud of the respect and trust farmers show him.

On one farmer's kitchen table was a letter from a lawyer employed by a Noongar family, positioning them as Native Title negotiators. Uncle Lomas laughed, but he didn't respect the traditional authority of these claimants, and he was angry. The farming couple were worried, and Uncle Lomas felt for them. They said they thought they'd always had a good relationship with 'the natives'.

Uncle Lomas didn't react, but it startled me, the sudden reversion to 'us and them' implicit in the language of the farming couple. The conversation had moved from division within the Noongar community to division between Noongars and wadjelas. Perhaps the 'us and them' mentality surfaced at the prospect of Noongars returning to the vicinity, especially those who came with lawyers talking Native Title.

'Us and them' — 'black against white' — seems an almost instinctive reflex in many people. Many Noongars have it too, of course, especially those whose identity has been so crucially formed by generations on the receiving end of racism; and that's most. It's like there are two worlds.

Kayang Hazel is not ignorant of the historical context of stolen land and racist injustice yet, like her brother Lomas, she's also able to see people as individuals rather than only as members of racial or political groups. A lack of political sophistication, or an excess of humanity? I reckon it's their strong connection to a traditional Indigenous heritage, *and* their participation — albeit on 'white' terms — in the workforce that enables them to be like this.

Many find themselves stranded between two worlds. The lawyer and writer Terri Janke has a poem, 'Between Two Worlds' which concludes:

> *My dark ancestors lay a silver blanket over me*
> *In the moonlight, but in life they had nothing to give*
> *Nothing that was not already taken*

The last time they slept on the sand
The last time I stepped off a plane

Two worlds, distant from one another and characterised by loss. 'Two World One', a poem by Janke's contemporary, Richard Frankland, also has a persona who inhabits two worlds, and concludes optimistically:

I'm a two world one
I can see inside two worlds
But one day I'll only have to see in one

That's the possibility I saw in what Kayang Hazel and Uncle Lomas were revealing to me. Rather than moving from one world to the other — the 'us and them' — their heritage and sense of place make it one world, and at worst they need only move, generously, from one polemical position to the other, even if only to see what it looks like from there. Uncle Lomas felt sorry for those farmers who felt threatened.

Here in the south of Western Australia our colonial history's racial and economic imperatives have made it very unusual to meet someone who is not either stranded in one of two worlds, or stretched between them.

Maya wangin

I once did a public reading with John Mateer, a poet of South African origin living in Australia. Prior to our performance, he very courteously sent me a copy of his latest volume, *Loanwords*, and when we met, moments before going on stage, he told me he was going to read a certain poem, 'In the Presence of a Severed Head'. In many ways it's a fine poem, probably intended as a kind of homage and a way of engaging with Western Australian colonial history, however it was the very poem in the collection that most perturbed me, mainly because of its use of Noongar language and concepts as recorded by various colonial authorities, and as I sat beside him on stage I was mortified to hear him utter:

Yagan, even you were re-incarnated — a white man! — once.

It's an idea in the early writings of the Swan River Colony: Noongar people on the west coast called the colonists *djanga*, a dialect variation of *djaanak*, and the diarists say it means the spirits of returned ancestors. I think it must've been used to describe those seemingly damaged, not quite human and deathly pale beings who'd so recently arrived in significant numbers. Spirit creatures. Devils maybe. The use of such a term, and the possibility that they may be filial relations, probably stems from the belief that any life form must inevitably be in some way a manifestation of the land's spirit. It's also an idea which was — and is — used to rationalise non-Indigenous occupation, and which often gets confused with reincarnation.

I find it difficult to explain why I felt so terrible at that particular reading, although the perpetuation of that very convenient notion of reincarnation was definitely one reason. Another was the realisation that there are very few forums for Noongar people to come to terms with the ideas of their ancestors and how they are represented in the archives, and so it can feel doubly wrong when relatively recent arrivals use those representations for their own purposes. In this instance, I was the sole Noongar representative, and it was particularly uncomfortable.

However, most disturbing was hearing the Noongar words of the poem read aloud. I had only been learning Noongar language for a short time myself, and admit that I, along with many others, still don't adequately know the world view and language of my Indigenous ancestors, but it was very unsettling to hear Noongar words and phrases spoken without reference to any other authority than the spellings available in the archives. It didn't sound much like any Noongar language I'd ever heard.

Noongar language is endangered. It's hard to find fluent speakers, and although its community is attempting to consolidate and regenerate both it and the ways of thinking embedded therein, it remains a difficult and continuing project. Additionally, I think it's important that if such language is to be shared so that all might more fully understand the extent of the human relationship with this country — then it must first be consolidated and rejuvenated in its home community before it is disseminated further.

Noongars have been disempowered by colonial history, and I don't think it helps any Noongar to hear a stranger using our ancestors' language badly when that language is still not available to so many of us.

I'd been attempting to learn Noongar for some time before I started working with Kayang Hazel. At one stage, when I was working at the Indigenous centre at a university, a few of us got together informally and sought the guidance of some competent speakers. For a time I attended classes in my suburb which were organised voluntarily. I pored over Noongar Language Centre publications, thumbed through all the available wordlists and dictionaries, borrowed tapes from various individuals, and went along to Education Department workshops designed to facilitate Noongar language teaching.

It wasn't easy learning Noongar, and not just because of the usual difficulties of learning any language, let alone an endangered one for which there are scarce resources and support.

For one thing, the nagging awareness of how important language is to identity, and the questions of how and why one cannot in fact speak it, generate insecurities. Some say the language was lost, while others insist it was stolen, but there is the taint of shame in either case: why didn't my family fight harder to retain it?

Another obstacle is that Noongar language is increasingly seen as cultural capital: in some circumstances it may be an important component of cultural exchange, a way of positioning individuals to become cultural brokers and representatives of their people, and may thus result in jealousies and rivalries. The existence of different dialects can exacerbate such tensions.

There's also the fact that, since many words of Noongar

obviously refer to nature, articulating the presence of such things as traffic and sirens, or the process of washing dishes or even operating an ATM, can be very challenging, even alienating. Mouthing sounds intrinsic to our geographical region, but strange at the same time, can make you feel as if you have stepped out of the contemporary world of traffic and ATMs, and are describing them from some other vantage point.

To the extent that the archives and other paper sources are relied upon, there is also the problem of the English alphabet's inadequacy at capturing Noongar sounds, and the problem of trusting the original transcribers. How accurate — how authentic — are the sounds being produced?

As I tried to indicate earlier, there are also sensitivities as to one's right to be learning Noongar. This doesn't apply only to wadjelas, but sometimes to those without elders and family who have carried and maintained the language.

So, for these reasons and more, I was thrilled when Kayang Hazel said she'd teach me our language. I tried to be systematic, and extracted examples of Noongar from the tapes we'd so far done, analysed the sounds she used, learned which letters of the international phonetic alphabet were appropriate, and laid them over some of the available word lists and dictionaries to see how well they fitted. I organised words into different categories, and we recorded her reading them so I could practise alone. Sometimes these exercises jogged her memory, and some fragment or phrase emerged that she thought was gone forever.

But I couldn't really insist on being too systematic. Kayang Hazel preferred to tell stories, sometimes heaping them one on another, along with lots of gossip and anecdotes. She recited detailed genealogies and complex connections, and offered insights into a distinctive perspective of our colonial history.

She had described people making smoke to mark a journey from Jerdacuttup to Cocanarup, a journey to their death. She told me about hearing our old people calling from within the smoke of a small ceremony near the head of a narrow river that, like many along the south coast, comes to a halt among the dunes of a sandy beach.

Only after a lot of rain do such rivers reach the ocean.

Midjal means rain: soft, misty rain. It can also mean tears.

'Kayep weliny,' said Kayang Hazel. *Water running.* The second word is the word for 'crying' and, in a curious similarity to English, the two words together could even be translated as 'water welling'. A lovely sound, and there was life in it, I thought, if I could let it run through me.

*

Maya wangin.

That's the wind talking, sounds coming on the wind, sort of. Like, if you say 'Noongar maya wangin,' that's the sound of Noongar talk.

And you know, Kimmy, lot of times, when we've lost someone, someone's been killed or hurt, I think of this story — not Daddy, but old Henry Dongup and Aunty Ellie and Grandfather Moses and them used to tell it — about people coming back, you know, like coming back to life. I'm wishing for it I s'pose, that it was like that.

They used to say it in language, making a sound — *wool, wool, wool* — like a wind, or a whirlwind, a willy-willy. Something like that.

There was this Noongar boy, see — well, maybe a man — but he was on his own, anyways. Mighta been *iernang, barnap* — an orphan, he got no family.

Anyway, he was camping, lying down between his fires. They used to use more than one fire; two little fires. Lying there, head back, looking up at the stars, thinking. Telling himself about the stories there, maybe. Listening to sounds in the night.

Hears this funny thing. A strange noise. Old people used to say 'dooyf' or 'dongorl'. But it coulda been an alarm clock, or a mobile phone. Mobile phone woulda been a strange noise back then, unna?

He can't help himself, see. He wants to know what it is. He sneaks away from the fire to have a look. *Waniny*, they say, walking like a woman when she's digging. Digging with her wana, you know. Waniny is sort of going along bent over, creeping along.

Getting up close, he sneaks along on his belly. Suddenly sees these great big feet, and he stops. Looks up. Oh! This great big monster. Djaanak yok koomba. *Devil woman.* A great big devil woman, horns on her head. Pale, grey like a ghost. Mob of them, a family of djaanak.

They whack him with a club, boy. Knock him out. Pick him up, carry him over to the fire and build up a big bonfire. When it's burned down a bit they throw him on it and cook him, like a roast, all the fat running out of him. Poke him with a stick, his skin coming off, crackling.

They eat him. No, no, just the mother ate him; she chased the others away. All the grease running down her chin. Usually djaanak got no manners, but this one is tidy. Fussy, fussy sort of eater. She eats the meat off the leg, puts the bone back on the fire. Same place where it got cooked.

Sometimes she throws a piece to one of her kids creeping back to get a feed. She makes them do the same, put the bone back where it come from.

Mmmm, eating. This bit, next bit. All of 'em put the bones back neat. Keep eating.

They finish. Mother one, she can hardly stand up 'cause her belly's so big. They walk away.

Gone.

Bones lying there, covered in ash, and ash blowing around a little bit. You can sorta see the body, the skeleton I mean. The spine all the way along. It looks a bit like a little grave, bones just covered. Ash moving ...

There! Near the mouth. Just like his tongue was moving, a few ashes circling around his mouth, his lips. Like a little willy-willy there, and the ashes spinning round and round.

Ashes spinning.

His head's sitting right there, just above the ground, like balanced and coming out of the little willy-willy.

Head, and his neck too.

Whirlwind getting bigger all the time, see. Slowly coming, coming like magic.

Bool wool nyin. *Alive*. There's different ways to say it, but it was like magic.

Anyway, yeah, bit by bit, until he's standing there, he's back alive again. Grabs his things, and off he goes. Gunna find his family, see.

That story ... about the old people at Cocanarup and that, unna? You think? About them still being there? Coming back to life? His tongue started it, see. Brought him back to life.

See, *woolalan*. That's like, light. Like first thing in the morning, or when you walk into a clearing

So, *wirna wooliny* ... light and wind, together. Spirit too.

*

After the story of the massacre, this was one of the first stories Kayang told me. The Noongar magically appearing, there! Reborn, regenerating in a small whirlwind of ash and smoke from the energy created by his tongue.

It's an exciting story for anyone, not least of all a writer preoccupied with the limits and power of language, yet Aunty Hazel told this story of regeneration so casually, skipping over a whole list of body parts she might have named, and offering alternative phrases for the sense of reappearance, of coming into being.

Yeah, Kayang Hazel said, she'd teach me Noongar language. Uncle Lomas talked about *wirn*, one of the words for spirit. He said we knew all about the Holy Spirit long before the white man came along.

He and Kayang Hazel helped me attempt the sound of Noongar, a sound very difficult to render on the page, but which helps me think of my family history differently. Sometimes it's as if, learning to make the sounds, I remake myself from the inside out. As if, in making the sounds of the language of this land, I make myself an instrument of it. As if, in uttering such sounds and making such meanings, I not only introduce myself to ancestors named Winnery, but beckon them closer to me.

While we were writing this book two of Kayang Hazel's brothers died, and so did a lot of her nephews, nieces and grandchildren.

Driving alone to a funeral in Gnowangerup I listened to tapes Kayang Hazel and I had made, and mouthed the sounds of Noongar language. I'd learned an old Noongar funeral song, a song our ancestors would have sung, and which was very similar to a text in the foreword of a Noongar language dictionary I'd been studying.

In the dictionary the song is called 'Hut Building Song', and it describes making a hut of leaves and twigs. The song I'd learned, while similar, ended with a line which translates literally as something like, 'What for this family-death?'

I sang that song for almost the whole drive to Gnowangerup, and as I drove, the bush I travelled through changed in character.

Noongars talk about how different trees mark different country. Different country, and somewhat different peoples too. Kayang said her dad used to receive message sticks in stamped envelopes; old forms utilising a new system. The type of wood was itself part of the message, indicating the region from where it had been cut and sent. Today, even in a speeding car, and even though the trees are mostly squeezed between fence and road or stand in isolated clumps within the paddocks, you can still see the country change as you travel.

Parking a little up the road from the church, I watched people milling around its entrance and greeting one another. They embraced, shook hands.

I joined the end of the crowd filing in, and took an empty pew at the very back of the church, feeling conspicuous.

Wadjela Noongar.

Kayang's grand-daughter Milana came and sat beside me.

We sang hymns, and afterwards went to the hall for sandwiches and tea. Kayang told me to bring two chairs over to the end of the trestle table upon which food was spread, and she sat me down next to her, and introduced me to more people than I could remember. Relations, she kept saying. Family.

Funerals are always sad, of course, but they also bring people together and provide a chance to consolidate and regroup even as death takes another away.

Gathering of Wilomin Noongar people, 2012.
Hazel Brown is seated in the centre.
(Photo courtesy of Wirlomin Noongar Language and Stories Project)

A very regional perspective

There's a bird, what our people call Nyoorrlem.

This is a big bird, a big owl. I wish I could show you one, wish I could find one. I only ever seen one in my life, but I've heard 'em.

Me and my mum and dad, we were working for the Nichols then, burning off, top end of Nichol's there, and Dad said, 'Oh, let's go for *koomal* then.' You know, possum.

I had the gun. We went to this big dry tree, big dry tree standing in the paddock. Oh, this big tree like that, boy. And course, I'm looking for tracks now, I'm looking for tracks.

When a possum climbs up a tree, his claws go deep into the tree, but when he's coming down the tree, he slides. He go so far, and then he jump.

I said, 'Oh, koomal in this tree.' Big tree it was, too.

Daddy said, 'I don't think so. I think something else in this tree.'

'I'll show you,' I said, and I grabbed the stick he had in his hand and started hitting the tree with it.

Daddy said, 'That's not a koomal track, come away from there, otherwise … You'll soon see what it is, you'll know all about it.'

I took no notice, see. I kept on hitting the tree. I wanted to get the koomal to come out. 'Cause sometimes, when you hit the tree, if possum's awake, well, he come to have a look and see what's going on.

And then this big thing come out, boy. I could see the big hole in the tree, big hole.

It just come out, head first. Went and stood out on a limb. About three feet high, long legs and big feet. Sorta short wings, and the face! Boy, his face was just like a man. And a pinchy nose. He had eyebrows and whiskers and a long neck. Down the front was just white, and on the sides it was a pretty pinkish colour, you know.

He looked down at us, and you see these big brown eyes just looking at you, and the feet. And whiskers even, and the wind blowing the whiskers. Looked as if to say, 'I don't mess with you fellas.'

You know I nearly died. 'Oh,' I said, 'shoot it, shoot it.' But Daddy said, 'No, you can't do that. He's not harming you. He's been here for a long time. He belongs to here. That's a Nyoorrlem. He's half-man. You can't touch him.'

He just give one shout, and flew straight up with his legs hanging down. I shut my eyes, didn't bother to know where it went.

Well, I just totally lost all interest in the possum after that.

I never stopped at that place in the night ever since. And I never ever go hunting in that corner. Nobody ever go hunting that way, 'cause that's Nyoorlem country.

If you come on it by chance, or you was tooken for it, and if you saw it once, I doubt very much if you'd want to go back and have a look for it again.

After dark, if you're messin' around in the bush getting *bardi*, they'll follow you home.

Another time, we were down towards Wellstead, down towards the hills.

There used to be a lot of *damar* there, years ago, a bit like those quokkas they got at Rottnest. Nothing now, they all finished.

This old man named Kingston had this farm, and we camped about mile and a half out.

So my cousins Lexie and Clara and myself, and another two cousins, and Cilla, and one of Dad's cousins, Cathy — us girls were looking for bardi now, thinking to go and get some *kamak*. It must've been about three o'clock.

Well, Aunty Ellie said, 'If you're gunna go, make sure you come back before sundown.'

'What for, why?'

'Well, you'll know all about it if you don't get back before sundown. I don't wanna tell you why, but you shouldn't go. This is not you fellas' place. You fellas strangers to this place, you gotta understand that, you're only visitors here. If you belong to this district it'd be different for you fellas, but … you want to go I can't stop you. I'll let you fellas go, but if you don't come back before sundown, you fellas know all about it.'

Well, off we went. Getting all the bardis, biggest lot of

bardis out. Pushing the trees down and getting them all. Oh, and there was a lot of kamak on the trees there too. We picking all the kamak there and having a good feed and looking around, messing around. We lost track of time, and hey, look, well it was well and truly after sundown.

And we gotta walk about a mile. And when we coming home, boy, it's dark. It's dark. We come home, carrying the bardi and all. Carrying all the bardi home, and everybody quiet, and looking around, and coming along in a group all bunched up.

Well as soon as we come home there, Aunty Ellie said, 'I told you fellas. You're not gunna have a sleep tonight. They're gunna come for you fellas. You had no right to stay there, that's their place, that's not your place.'

Well, you know, about half past eight, nine o'clock in the night, I'm lying in the front of the tent, and I can hear 'em coming, shouting, 'Nyoo-ef, nyoo-ef, nyoo-ef,' like that. I crawled right in the foot side of Mummy and Daddy and I nearly suffocated myself, yeah? I tell you what, I never got out of that bed til next day.

Anyways, next day old Grandfather Dongup said, 'C'mon, I'll take you fellas and I'll show you fellas. You think this is not their place, this is a Nyoorrlem place. They'll follow and find you no matter where you go, you know. They'll find you.'

So he took us back.

Well, Uncle Clancy wouldn't come, Cilla backed off, it was me, Clara, Lexie and … and Charlie, he come. Charlie. And we went back with Grandfather Dongup to the foot of the hill, walked right through the scrub. Oh lovely. Walked to the foot of the hills, and a big cave, a big cave like a big *kornt*, like a big *maya-maya* right in the side of the hill there. And just black right back inside. Just dark.

And in the front, Kim, true, in the front you see where they was eating the bardi. All the heads, and bits of bardi laying here and there. And way further back you see all the bones of little animals. I don't think they were meat eaters, so might be dingoes, I don't know.

Grandfather said, 'Now you fellas, this is their place, and you fellas don't come to this place anymore.'

Come to that place! I couldn't wait to get away from it! I never went back to that place!

Years ago we used to get very scared. Matter of fact, even now, I don't go to a place where I was told not to go when I was young. Even to the hills now, Kimmy. We never ever go into the hilly country — all along the ranges, and the Stirling Ranges — because that really is not our place.

Any time you go hunting in that area, you know, if you wanna go to the toilet in the night, never let anybody stop the motor. Frightening thing you know.

When we were out staying in the Needilup area I never ever heard of them, you know, Nyoorrlem. But they reckon they mostly in the hilly country, you know. And they always like tall timbered country, I dunno why. I never ever heard of them anywhere else, you know.

That place belongs to the people that lived there. That's not anyone else's. Even from Borden, you never catch people go hunting there. Not unless they was in a group, they might go into a paddock. But no-one would ever go and explore those ranges. You never know what might be waiting for you there.

That's where they reckon the little people mostly live around there. Hilly country. Little mamara men, you know.

*

It's a very regional perspective Kayang Hazel offers; only a relatively small part of the continent is home, and beyond that you need introductions and the welcome of its people. Obviously, it's too simple to say 'the bush' is home. There are many different homes, which is another reminder that a single Indigenous Australia is only a political construct, a consequence of colonisation.

Prior to an expanding frontier, interaction between different Indigenous groups was most likely by way of exchange, ceremony, negotiation and intermarriage. Today, interaction between different groups often occurs within infrastructure basically shared with the wider society, and negotiation often takes place within the constraints of bureaucracy. This can sometimes make it awkward to protect and consolidate regional knowledge, and ensure that the people who possess that knowledge, the custodians, are consulted — rather than decisions being made only by the significant members of an Indigenous bureaucracy — the power brokers. This is a concern for Kayang Hazel and the Roberts family, as well as other families of the region. It's a difficult and thorny issue, how to ensure that the right people speak for country.

Uncle Lomas asked me to accompany him to the south coast for a men's camp organised by one of the family, Graeme Miniter, but first we had to honour an invitation to a local university's Aboriginal bridging course graduation ceremony. Uncle Lomas and one of his nephews, Jason Miniter, who was graduating, had been asked to participate in the ceremony. From the small crowd, I watched Jason wave a smoking branch of the mangart tree over each student as Uncle Lomas shook their hand and said, 'Karam, nyoondok winyan. Yey, nyoondok moordidjabiny.'

Recently, you were weak. Now, you are becoming strong.

By eight-thirty that night we were climbing the hills at the edge of the city, driving to Quaalup in the rain.

We turned off the bitumen at around two in the morning. Rain was a constant diagonal grain in the headlights, and the road a sheet of water and mud. I was driving, and only luck prevented us crashing as we drifted, slid, skimmed along.

We turned off again and followed two sandy wheel ruts as the scrub closed in around us and scraped the sides of the car.

Jason stepped out of the car into fine, drizzling rain to open a gate and our headlights picked out a huddle of tents and huts and a canopy under which someone sat beside the camp fire. 'James Brown,' Jason said, and the name almost made me look around for the American soul singer. Uncle Lomas held out his hand, used the intimate name, 'Udel'.

We sat talking around the fire for a short time, before Graeme Miniter stumbled into the smoke in his shirt and underpants, yawning and rubbing his tousled head, standing so tall in the darkness I saw the aptness of his nickname — Boomer — a big old male kangaroo.

Daylight already diluting the darkness, we lay on the floor of a hut among a dozen or so others in blankets and sleeping bags. Udel was talking non-stop. He had a lot to talk about.

'Cancer,' he said, and laughed. 'You go to the doctor feeling fine, and he says six months. What's a man meant to do? They want me to give up drinking and smoking, but I'm gunna die anyway, aren't I?' Strange to say, we were laughing with him. Cancer. What else can you do but laugh, find some relief that way?

The next morning, crouching under the sweep of peppermint trees at a little sandy break in the bank of the estuary, I slipped mullet from a net we'd set late the night before. Kayang Hazel says mullet is *meradong*, and calls it her grandmother's kin.

Later in the day we followed the rabbit-proof fence to where it stops at a cliff above the sea. Some of us scrambled part of the way down a rocky cliff to fish for groper. A swell broke against the cliff base, drenching the fishers. I was one of those few wary souls who stayed high and dry.

Back at camp we sat around a fire. Thin smoke curled around us, and the fine misty rain gathered at the edge of the canvas canopy above our heads and fell slowly, like tears.

On another trip Uncle Lomas showed me one of the old people's graves, marked by stones. A rust and iron-oxide sort of colour — ironstone, I think it's called — they look like conglomerations of gravel.

The grave was a depression in the earth, filled with the rocks. I thought about Fanny Winnery's grave, and all the graves of those before her. I remembered Kayang Hazel's story of the Noongar spirit coming back to life, and how you could see the bones and skeletal pattern of a Noongar within the mound of ash.

There's a lot of four-wheel driving at some of these south-coast men's camps. Everyone crowds into a few vehicles, and it's up and down through sand dunes, and along crisp white beaches as the white sand squeals under the tyres. We're looking into the waves for salmon. We stop, and there's a rush to grab rods and get the lines into the ocean.

Uncle Lomas says he's never fished for salmon in his life. They used to fish the estuaries, and walk everywhere. Not that he minds a four-wheel drive, or fishing for salmon. He showed me where the old time Noongar Jack Waini leapt from a cliff onto a big old groper floating on the ocean's surface far beneath him. They say he grabbed it and wrestled it to dry land.

We saw the sand blowing in the sea breeze, and followed the way our Bobby Roberts led the more famous J S Roe through the constantly shifting dunes.

We visited the site where Wilba stood chest-deep in the ocean to lure the great shark close enough for him to spear it.

The light was thickening as we drove back to camp. A couple of small kangaroos stood tall among the mallee, ears up and forearms held diffidently at their chests. With their windows wound down, our shooters sat with their bums on the window ledge, their feet inside and rifles resting on the vehicle's roof.

Shots sounded loud in the soft liquid light, echoed several times.

The boys — teenagers — dragged the kangaroos back to the vehicles.

My previous experience of hunting along the south coast was as a boy in the late 1960s, and all the shooters were drunk. The baying voices, the gushing of vomit and blood, the stabbing light and deep shadows had sent me away that time. This was different, even though there were cars and guns, and even though I still prefer the cunning and craft of snares, perhaps because that sort of hunting seems a metaphor for study and writing. Bool wool ngadanginy. A careful, almost magical, hunting.

That evening we ate *yongar datj*. Ngalak yongar datj ngaaniny.

There was sustenance; in the meat and in the words too — in the making of these sounds in the land of our ancestors.

Only a little Noongar language fits in this book, since it's the sound that matters to me, and print does no justice to that.

Eduardo Galeano, playing with translations from other languages into English, has spoken of paper as the 'skin of God'. What writers do, he said, is deal with the skin of God. We write messages on it, which we send to our friends — many of whom we do not yet know — and we embrace them with our language.

The usual Noongar word for paper is *bibool,* taken from one dialect's word for paperbark tree. Paperbark trees often stand beside *bily*, our dialect's word for river, which is almost the same as the word for navel. The earth around them is called *boodjar*, and to be pregnant is to be *boodjari*.

Whichever way we put it, writing — to be a writer — is to offer sustenance and life. It is also, as in so many matters of creation and fertility, about intimacy.

Sometimes we sat with a tape-recorder between us, its spools rolling. I've imagined similar scenes in my fiction as conversation. The reality was different, because Kayang Hazel's poor hearing made it mostly a monologue. I didn't mind, and transcribing her words locked her mind with mine.

She listened on headphones to my attempts at speaking Noongar, recordings of my voice uttering the sounds she'd given me.

Ngalang Noongar maya wanginy. *Speaking our Noongar sound.*

One day, as Kayang Hazel and I sat in her front room with the tape-recorder, shuffling papers we'd collected, one of her grandchildren, Ryan Brown, came visiting with some others of the family. Kayang Hazel showed them a photo of an Aboriginal man with his people in chains, and started telling them about old Bobby Roberts.

Not an easy story with which to begin.

Next, she picked up a Noongar word list we'd compiled, and began reading it aloud, elaborating stories on each word.

Ryan later said, as many have, that he never valued this sort of knowledge when he was younger. Never realised how important it was.

No, how could we?

And they all want to know about it now, he said, referring to people outside of the family.

There are few elders left with the knowledge Kayang Hazel and her siblings carry, and I — the some-say ghost-of-a-Noongar — had written at least some of it down, and — in turn — some of that is in this book.

Ryan agreed with me that it'd be good if a few of us got together and went through some of the material his grandmother had given us, particularly the word list and tapes Kayang and I had made.

'Yes,' Kayang Hazel said. 'Yeah, you do that.'

We faltered a little.

I'm ashamed to say it didn't really happen. Maybe we couldn't arrange our time well enough, maybe we had too many distractions. I was busy with some other work I'd taken on, Ryan got into some trouble, Ed Brown got really sick, Jason Miniter got a new job, Graeme Miniter was too far away, and working. We were living in different towns, or spread apart in the city. We were trying to keep the Wilomin Aboriginal Corporation functioning.

Kayang Hazel and her brother and sister wanted to get some land in traditional country. I could see the sense of that, since I'd seen how the land ignited their memories, and how language and culture and place went together; sometimes, like at Hunter River, a place demands a certain song. Often there's a certain place for bush tucker, and the words for that food and the harvesting of it make best sense right there. Rocks can set a narrative in motion, animate the stone. I thought, too, of how we could re-establish a presence in traditional country and consolidate the networks these elders had in the rural community. And with land we could formalise cultural consolidation and rejuvenation in such a way as to prepare younger members of our family-community to take on roles in partnership

— at least — with land rehabilitation organisations and tourist and cultural enterprises, in such a way that, rather than ceding rights and authority, they enhanced them.

To gain a land base we had to enter into the labyrinthine bureaucratic requirements of the Indigenous Land Corporation, and the South West Aboriginal Land and Sea Corporation.

Thinking in such a political and strategic way, you end up moving in a different direction altogether, though perhaps we can eventually circle around again, and remain oriented to an ancestral heritage and home.

Writing is still a relatively new thing to Noongar people, although people like Rosemary van den Berg, Alf Taylor and Richard Wilkes, among others are all published writers. I think we know its value. I'm often tempted to think some of our old people sought out anthropologists, linguists and historians to help them preserve what they knew for future generations.

Pa Tjinjel wasn't so enthusiastic, however. In fact, according to Kayang Hazel her father was reluctant to pass on his knowledge and language, and wary of any who came seeking it. Luckily for us he changed his mind when he was a very old man. They reckon he was a hundred years old when he died, which means he must've been about eighty-five when Kayang Hazel started making notes.

He'd been very badly burned in an accident and, after recovering, always felt so cold that he'd need a fire constantly beside him. Kayang Hazel gave me the tattered notes left from what she'd scribbled in those last years of his, and I like to think they were passed to me from some impervious place at the centre of flames and smoke.

So Kayang Hazel and I wrote this with the support of her siblings, Lomas Roberts and Audrey Brown, just so we could think about and share something of the people who were already along the southern part of Western Australia when the boats first came, about what's happened since, and where we might go next. Of course, a book is not enough to do that and we haven't got enough readers among our own people, but even in colonised south-western Australia there are messages left in rock, and stories to be read from the land itself.

Hazel Brown.

Lomas Roberts.   *Audrey Brown.*

(Photos c. 2008 courtesy of Wirlomin Noongar Language and Stories Project)

Eaglehawk Country

Audrey and me camped at Bremer. We went with Graeme, my grandson. He had the video camera.

'What area you wanna do first?' I said.

'Oh, we'll do Cape Riche. Cape Riche area.'

We photographed the places: the beach where they used to spear the salmon, where we used to watch 'em spearin' salmon; all the camp sites; the old soaks; and the corroboree ground especially, where the Noongars would camp.

You could see remains of periwinkle shells and different shellfish, and you could see the ashes of their fires. Audrey showed him too.

And Graeme said, 'How you know Noongars camped here, Granny?'

I said, 'When you see green moss, green moss growing, you get a stick and you dig up the moss, and sometimes you find bones or shells, and that's where they camped.' I showed him this was where so-and-so camped, and this was where we camped, and this is where they corroboree.

From there we went back towards Boat Harbour, so I said, 'Go down here, and I'll show you something.'

Audrey said, 'What?'

I said, 'I'll show you waterhole, fresh waterhole.'

Audrey said, 'Girl,' she said, 'there's no fresh water here. Me and Ray come here many times, there's no fresh water here. We always have to take our water.'

I said, 'Yeah, I'll show you where the water is.'

She said, 'Oh, you poor fella.' They was laughing, pointing at their heads, see, saying I'm going mad, *kaatwara*.

Anyway, we got to the place. Graeme tried to fish, and couldn't catch a fish. Big bream swimming around, but he had stinking bait, and they wouldn't bite.

I said, 'I'm going for a walk. When you fellas come down, pull up round the corner over there,' I said.

About, oh, half an hour after, they come behind. I went and had a drink of their water, and then I said, 'Waste that water now, and we'll get some fresh water, clean water for us.'

'Can't waste this water, this is the last water we got.'

'Of course you can waste it.'

'Where you gunna get fresh water from?'

I said, 'I'll show you where there's water.'

Audrey said, 'Oh, you winyan poor fella,' she said. 'You got no brains.' And she said, 'Never knew she been in a mental home.'

Any rate, we get in the motor and drove along to the creek. I said, 'Pull up here Graeme.' Graeme stopped. They looked at one another.

I said, 'Get your camera.'

He asked me, 'What for?'

'Take a photo of the waterhole.'

He got the camera. They both looking, laughing at me.

I wasted the water out of the two containers. And we come along. I'm walking in the front, following a pad.

I said, 'This here's a kangaroo pad; you see all these kangaroo tracks? What you think this kangaroo's goin' this way for?'

Audrey said, 'Must be gunna cross river, I don't know why.'

I said, 'He's going to drink water.'

She said, 'Oh he's gunna be one thirsty kangaroo then, 'cause there's no water in here to drink.'

So when we walk out on the hill there, and we got on the cliff, I said to Graeme, 'What's that down there?'

See, at the top end there's a big high bank, and fresh water's on this side, and salty water's on that side. Salty water can't come up this way, but the fresh water can go down that way. You can see the difference in the water. Close up, you can see like tadpoles on this side, but on that side you see nothing. That's where fish come up, see.

Graeme looked at it. And Graeme looked at Audrey. Graeme sniffed and said, 'How you know this was here?' He said, 'That's fresh water.'

I said, 'Yeah, that's fresh water. But that's not all.'

So we walked down the rock there. All the weeds were all banked up, it was just like a big dam, see, from top end of the river. But because it was all scrubby people never come this way, see. They fish down the bottom there.

It's concealed, see. From the cliff, you can't tell. And

underneath, down the bottom, there's a big ngamar hole right around like that boy, and it's about, must be over six feet deep and the water's just blue. And it's fresh as a daisy.

Audrey reckoned, 'Oh, this is salt water.'

I said, 'You ever see tadpoles swimming in salt water, eh? All right, take the photo now.'

Graeme sat down on a rock.

'You know years ago this was where they used to camp, when they travelling, when they run away from police. This is where they used to always stay,' I said.

'And you see that red rock over on the other side, over there? That red rock?'

Graeme nodded his head.

'Years ago,' I said, 'little *woodatji*, like a little tiny bloke, he was here. Well they used to live in the hills. One day they all had a big fight, so the story goes, and the family went away and left behind one little bloke. He was by himself, see? He come here looking for his family.

'When he come along, he had an idea there was water here, and he sat down on this rock, and he was looking across to the cave over there. He could see people walking around over there, and they were his own people, too.

'He was sitting here,' I said. 'Right here. This is the rock he was sitting on.'

And Graeme said, 'How you know he was sitting on this rock?'

'Well,' I said, 'he left his footmarks down for you to see.'

I broke the bushes like that, and I swept the sand away from the rock, and you could see it, two little footprints. Each little foot about that long — about five inches long — and the big toe sticking out, and the five little toes, and the foot, the heel mark and all.

I said, 'That's where he was sitting, watching all the others and that.'

Graeme said, 'Just fancy that,' and he took a photo of it.

'He sat down and he watched them,' I said, 'with his arms folded, watching, see if they're gunna come and look at him, see? And this woman, she'd been following him behind, Noongar woman.

'That woman sneaked up behind him, and she stood on her left leg, with her right leg up. And her left foot went right in the muddy ground, and she hit him on the head with a stick, with her wana. He was in the wrong place, see. This wasn't his place.'

And Graeme and Audrey, they said, 'Well, how you know? Where's the woman's track?'

I said, 'You're standing on it.'

I cleaned more sand away, and showed them the woman's footprint, in the rock. Proper imprint, you know. Proper imprint. You could see how she stood on one leg, how the foot went down as she swung to hit him.

Then I covered it all up with sand, and I said, 'Don't you two show anybody this place. You're not supposed to, you know.'

We always cover it up with sand, because if you leave it everybody will see it, and everybody will want to go and see it, see. They'll make a sort of museum thing of it.

There's a lot of thick scrub there still. And some people say they're still there, those little men. You can feel their eyes watching you.

*

Transcribing this story, I realised it was about respect for cultural authority and traditional ownership, and that, like Graeme, I was being welcomed and warned at the same time.

And you, our reader?

Our colonial history consists of representations of Aboriginal people in the interests of non-Aboriginal Australia, of dispossession and damage in that cause. There's a pattern to it, and a similar texture in the archival history: FWMB! LFBA! The staccato sputtering of 'last full blood aboriginal' and 'first white man born' is trapped in the grid of hessian, stale and layered in the grooves of corrugated iron, and dried like blood on the barbed wire of stolen land. It's a very prickly fabric, this one of national identity.

There's something missing in the pattern, the texture, in the very material. We all need some other yarn.

It's about respect, Kayang had said. It's about being honest. I think our collective identity also resides in building respectful relationships.

I remember my first novel's biographical note — drafted well over ten years ago — referred to me as of Aboriginal and British descent. That was honest, as I understood it then.

Preparing the biographical note for my second novel I wrote: 'descended from people who lived on the south-east coast of Western Australia, and one among those who called themselves Noongar.' I intended to emphasise the authority of that community — those who call themselves Noongar — in confirming that identity. As I've said, it's a political stance. I'd only just met Kayang Hazel.

*'It's about respect': at a Perth metropolitan primary school,
2008. Standing: Roma Winmar, Kim Scott.
Seated: Iris Woods, Ed Brown Snr (Hazel's nephew).
(Photo courtesy of Wirlomin Noongar Language and Stories Project)*

Politics on its own is not enough. Aunty Hazel helped me understand that the place we live in is Noongar country. When I was younger I never knew of such places, such stories. With her I followed ancient footprints and knelt to drink from waterholes, felt my palms settle in smooth hollows in granite where many, many hands had rested. Making the sounds of Noongar country my thinner tongue-tip wavered by palate and teeth ridge, and my breath entered internal spaces I scarcely knew existed. It was as if I was being reshaped from the inside out and, standing alone and formless within smoke, I heard voices calling from all around me.

What is the significance of all this, other than to my own personal preoccupations?

Well, being part of countless generations and the societies that arose from here and nowhere else could be part of all our collective identities, our shared heritage. We might be part of a nation-state fused to its continent by Indigenous roots and blossoming arrivals.

Hard to imagine? Not once you take that liberating leap from polemics to story; that right to imagine and act on possibility.

The way to keep country and culture alive — and not like a museum — is to have its people welcoming and introducing others into its stories. We need health, strength and confidence to do that.

We're not there yet. After a shared history overwhelmingly characterised by the damage done to Indigenous people and to the land, I don't think its right to suddenly talk sharing and caring, as if it was all some sort of grand Indigenous eco-tourism experience.

Indigenous tourism, in fact, is an interesting example to think about, especially in the region and history we've been considering. Imagine being descended from people who lived here before colonisation only to have others — immigrants, tourists, *white* people — turn their back on you to visit sites you don't know, learn songs from an old language you didn't understand, pluck the fruits of country, and then return to a healthy affluence of which you have no part?

In order to help strengthen Indigenous communities — and that's the only means by which an Australian nation-state will have any chance of grafting onto Indigenous roots — we need some sort of 'gap' between Indigenous and non-Indigenous societies, a moratorium, a time of exclusion to allow communities to consolidate their heritages. After that, exchange and interaction from relatively equal positions should be possible, because that's how cultural forms are tested and grow.

We're not suggesting some nostalgic retreat to land or to some simple pre-colonial past. Early Noongars like Mokare, Bobby Roberts, Fred McGill and others provide, I think, inspiration — they were more than able to innovate and adapt. Looking only backwards won't work when Noongar society today has such a high proportion of young people, all of whom need to be reaching with confidence and enthusiasm beyond what they know.

No, what we're talking about is maintaining a heritage, consolidating a long presence in a place, and developing relationships. We mean expanding the Noongar world so that there is one world, not two, and no need to be stuck in or between one or the other.

Ed Brown rang. Had I heard from Kayang Hazel lately? He'd seen her walking down St Georges Terrace that morning, a city street parallel to the river which — bounded each side by skyscrapers — becomes a canyon for the howling desert wind of the morning, and the gusting sea breeze of the afternoon. Locked in peak-hour traffic, Ed couldn't stop, couldn't even call out. He thought she was heading for some government agency or department, maybe visiting a mining company, or calling on someone she knew in the High Court … Trying to get help for the family, get some land to rest in.

The image stayed with me: a wiry old woman, deaf to the snarling traffic, striding with a ferocious wind at her back across the alternating planes of shade and eye-watering sunlight laid out upon the city's concrete path.

*

There's different waterholes. Daddy used to say, 'Not only we travel this road you know. I travelled this road when I was a kid, and old people travelled before …'

You camped at the camp site, like the same area where they camped, but you made sure you never camped on top of their camp. But you travelled that same track, you know. I told you before.

All those old places are all fenced off now, but there's one place I'd really love to go back and see, that's Nornanap.

I remember this old road now, this old road where we used to go; there's this river, freshwater river … Up there at Nornanap there, that's where Dad and them used to get kangaroos. We camped there for a time. Swamp there on the side. There's one tree there, a big mo tree, had seven eaglehawk nests on it. Seven nests!

Seven eaglehawk nests on the one tree. They weren't little nests, they were big nests.

Eaglehawks flying everywhere. That's eaglehawk country. They call it Nornanap, and it's supposed to be snake country, but more eagles than anything else.

There's a little freshwater gully that Uncle Bob took me to, and going across it like that, about ten inches wide, there's like a reef of white quartz. And this water is trickling right over the top of white quartz. And you could see all pretty colours, boy.

Talk about gemstones. Oh, the prettiest place. Prettiest sight out, true.

And down the bottom, heaps of gilgies, one big claw, one little one, you know.

We used to go camping out there, stay there for about, oh, a week. Then light a fire behind like to burn all the scrub where they hunting so it'll be good hunting again next time, and then shift further down to another waterhole.

You know Kim, through the years I've listened to people, and I can't say that I haven't learned a lot from white people. But I have been educated Noongar way.

Now what I mean is, I know the rules of my people. And when I say I been educated Noongar way, I always believe that I have had the best education of all, you know. I think that we were well taught.

Respect, respect is everything. We always walk behind our elders, we never walk in front of any of our old people. When they were sitting down on the ground, or squatting down, or even having something to eat, we never crossed in front of them; we always walked behind them, never in front of them.

When we wanted anything, we always asked for it, we never ever took what didn't belong to us. If we needed anything, we always asked. And if elders said no, we couldn't have it, you accepted that, and you didn't go and steal it.

I remember years ago old Grandfather Moses teaching us, because Grandfather Moses was like our mentor, 'cause my own grandfather died in 1930 — he died two weeks after my own father died, so I was only five years of age. When I became about six or seven Mummy would always say, or Daddy would always say, 'Oh go and ask Grandfather Moses and he'll tell you.'

Old Grandfather, he explained to us about Noongar rules and about what you should do, and what you shouldn't do, and how if you cared for people you shared with people.

Say, if someone is in a big hole, you help them out. You reach down and you help them out.

Little orphan kids, they used to call 'em *barnap*, little lonely ones. That was our job when we were young. We always had to look after the little ones.

If the older people needed water or needed their fire made, then we used to have to go around and get the sticks and make their fire. Go down to the soak, or the dam, or the creek, and go and get water so the old people had their wood and their water and what they needed.

Grandfather always used to say, 'If you take what's not yours, what belongs to another people,' — he never used to say *other* people, he used to say *another* people — 'that's pinchin', that's stealing.'

There was a lot of people in our community, bush Noongars, that knew the bush, that you learned a lot from. And most of them are willing to talk, you know, and tell you things.

They're still there, you know, at the old places. Sometime I feel 'em, and I turn around expecting to see someone coming over the hill, coming out of the smoke.

Kim Scott with Kayang Hazel.
(Photos this page and next 2008, courtesy of
Wirlomin Noongar Language and Stories Project)

Glossary

Spelling generally follows that recommended by the Noongar Language and Cultural Centre's *Noongar Dictionary*, though the use of 'p' instead of 'b' and 't' instead of 'd', and a technique to show diphthongs, would do better justice to Kayang Hazel's dialect.

baal	he, she, it
barang	bush; get, grab, seize
bardi	grub
barnap	orphan
bibool	paperbark tree
bily	river, navel
boodjar	earth, sand, ground
boodjari	pregnant
bool	magic stone, magically. (This word seems able to be used in different ways. Kayang uses it with the word for get or grab, to mean stealing; thus, 'bool barang' is to steal. In 'bool wool ngadanginy' she uses it to mean 'sneaking up hunting,' a phrase also used by the Humphries family as evidenced in the Noongar Language Centre's publication, *Noongar Our Way*, where it is written as 'borl worl ngadanginy.' My ear is not sensitive enough to determine whether the 'r'

sound is always there or not, and it seems to vary with Kayang's use. Her deafness and refusal to wear a hearing-aid severely limited our discussion of something like this. See 'wool' for further discussion.)

daalak	promised one
damar	wallaby, like quokka (*also* tamar)
datj	meat
djaanak	devil
dowak	hitting stick
dwoort	dog (*also* dwert)
iernang	orphan
kaat	head
kaatwara	mad
kalari	yellow-tongued lizard
kamak	bush food, long berry found on vines
kanya	ashamed
karam	yesterday
karder	racehorse goanna (*also* kardar)
karlmaat	firestick
karwa	parrot
kayang	old woman, female elder
kayep	water
koomal	possum
koomba	big
kornt	hut (*also* maya-maya)
kwel	sheoak
mamang	whale
mamara	little people (*also* mamari)
mangart	jam tree
maya	sound (and similar to the word for liver)
maya-maya	hut (*also* kornt)
meradong	mullet
midjal	rain, tears

minditj	damaged, sick
mo	yate tree
moordidjabiny	becoming strong
moort	family; tree or bush
mulga	clever man with special powers (*also* malka)
ngalang	we, ours, with us
ngadanginy	hunting
ngaaniny	eating
ngalak	we
ngama	waterhole
ngari	salmon
ngaw	bird, mallee hen
ngoolak	black cockatoo (*also* ngoorlak)
nyoondok	you
nyoorlem	owl; devil-bird
wadjela	white person
wana	digging stick
wangin	talking (*also* wanginy)
waniny	creep along, walk like a woman digging
wardong	crow
weliny	welling, crying (*also* waliny)
wilo	curlew
wilyaworri	a type of grass
winyan	weak, poor fellow
wirn	spirit (in a sentence this word is sometimes said wirna)
woodadji	mischievous little fella
wool	lightly, barely visible (?) (I'm not confident about this word. Kayang used it in the phrase 'bool wool ngadanginy' to mean something like 'sneaking up hunting' (see note for *bool*). Tim McCabe, who worked extensively with Cliff Humphries and for whose language skills I have the utmost respect, has confirmed this sort of usage in conversation with me. Kayang also uses the word in the phrase 'wirna

wooliny' and reiteratively as 'wool wool wool' when she was talking about a spirit being re-formed. Uncle Lomas says 'woolo' is light.)

woolalan	light, light coming
worting	ant nest
yey	now
yok	woman
yongar	kangaroo

Bibliography

Arthur, Jay, 'Jay Arthur on Dictionaries of the Default Country', *Lingua Franca*, Radio National, ABC, 12 June 1999.

Bates, Daisy, *The Native Tribes of Australia*, Isobel White (ed.), National Library of Australia, 1985.

Bignell, Merle, *The Fruit of the Country*, University of Western Australia Press, 1977.

Bindon, P and Chadwick, R, *A Nyoongar Wordlist from the South-West of Western Australia*, West Australian Museum, 1992.

Birdsall, C and Brown, H, Untitled and unpublished transcripts (in authors' possession).

Brockway, Marion, 'The Dunns of Cocanarup', *Early Days* (1970), Vol 11, part 4, 1998.

Cameron, Anson, *Tin Toys*, Picador, 2000.

Cavanagh, Gordon James, Oral History OH 70, Battye Library, 1975.

Chalarimeri, Ambrose Mungula, *The Man from the Sunrise Side*, Magabala Books, 2001.

Coleman, Will, untitled and unpublished writings (in authors' possession).

Daniels, Spike, interviewed in Eades, A and Roberts, P, *Report on Documentation of Research into Aboriginal Involvement in the Land in the South-west Region of Western Australia*, Community Consultation for the Seaman Land Inquiry (unpublished), 1984.

Dench, Alan 'Nyungar', in *Macquarie Aboriginal Words,* Thieberger and McGregor (eds), Macquarie Library, 1994.

Dimer, Karl, *Elsewhere Fine,* self-published, Kalgoorlie, 1989.

Douglas, Wilfred H, *The Aboriginal Languages of the South-west of Australia,* Australian Institute of Aboriginal Studies, Canberra, 1976.

Eades, A and Roberts, P, *Report on Documentation of Research into Aboriginal Involvement in the Land in the South-west Region of Western Australia,* Community Consultation for the Seaman Land Inquiry (unpublished), 1984.

Fogarty, Lionel, *New and Selected Poems: Munaldjali, Mutuerjaraera,* Hyland House, 1995.

Foster, David, *In the New Country,* Fourth Estate, London, 1999.

Frankland, Richard, 'Two World One' in Josie Douglas (compiler), *Untreated: poems by black writers,* jukurrpa books, 2001.

Galant, Heather and Wanless, Bob, *History of Aborigines along the South Coast,* nd, (a report of historical documentation of Aborigines along the south coast of Western Australia and held in Ravensthorpe museum).

Galeano, Eduardo, 'In Defence of the Word' in *The Graywolf Annual Five: Multicultural Literacy,* Rick Simonson and Scott Walker (eds), Graywolf Press, Saint Paul, 1988.

Gifford, P, *Black and White and in Between: Arthur Dimer and the Nullarbor,* Hesperian Press, Perth, 2002.

Grant, Stan, *The Tears of Strangers: a memoir,* Harper & Collins, 2002.

Green, Neville, *Aborigines of the Albany Region, 1821–1898: The Bicentennial Dictionary of Western Australians,* University of Western Australia Press, 1989.

Green, Neville and Moon, Susan, *Far from Home: Aboriginal Prisoners of Rottnest Island, 1838–1931. Dictionary of Western Australians, Vol. X,* University of Western Australia Press, 1997.

Haebich, Anna, *For Their Own Good: Aborigines and government in the southwest of Western Australia 1900–1940,* University of Western Australia Press, Nedlands, WA, 1988.

Hassell, Cleve, *The Hassells: a history of the 'Hassells of Albany' covering primarily their activity as settlers in the 19th century,* C W Hassell, 1973.

———, *The Hassells of Albany*, C W Hassell, 1972.

Hassell, Ethel, *My Dusky Friends*, C W Hassell, 1975.

Hodge, Bob and Mishra, Vijay, *Dark Side of the Dream: Australian literature and the post colonial mind*, Allen & Unwin, 1991.

Janke, Terri, 'Between Two Worlds' in Douglas, Josie (compiler), *Untreated: poems by black writers*, jukurrpa books, 2001.

Lamperd, Laurel, paraphrase of an interview with Bill (Will) Coleman in Galant and Wanless, *History of Aborigines along the South Coast*, nd (held in Ravensthorpe museum).

Mallet, Kathleen, *To the Bar Bonded: A History of Early Marble Bar*, Hesperian Press, 1993.

Mateer, John, *Loanwords*, Fremantle Arts Centre Press, 2002.

Mulvaney, John and Green, Neville, *Commandment of Solitude: the journals of Captain Collet Barker 1828–1831*, Melbourne University Press, 1992.

Neville, A O, *Australia's Coloured Minority: its place in the community*, Currawong Publishing, Sydney, 1948.

Pearson, Noel, 'On the Human Right to Misery, Mass Incarceration and Early Death', the Dr Charles Perkins Memorial Lecture, 25 October 2001.

Police Occurrence Book, Ravensthorpe/Phillips River, 1901–1903, Battye Library.

Pyne, Stephen J, *Burning Bush: a fire history of Australia*, Holt, New York, 1991.

Rijavec, Frank (director), *A Million Acres a Year*, Snakewood Films, 2002.

Rintoul, John, *Esperance Yesterday and Today* (4th edn), Perth, 1986.

Roe, J S, *Exploration Diaries 1846–57*, Vol. 4, Battye Library.

Russell, Lynette *A Little Bird Told Me: family secrets, necessary lies*, Allen & Unwin, 2002.

Standley, Ethel, correspondence (held in Ravensthorpe Museum).

Von Brandenstein, C G, *Nyungar Anew*, Pacific Linguistics Series C-99, Department of Linguistics, Research School of Pacific Studies, Australian National University, 1988.

Whitehurst, Rosie (compiler), *Noongar Dictionary*, Noongar Language and Cultural Centre, 1997.

Newspapers

Albany Advertiser, 31 December 1930.

Australian Advertiser, 30 July 1888; 19 June 1893; 18 and 19 November 1889.

Inquirer, 6 April, 9 May, 12 June 1877; 8 July 1879.

Inquirer and Commercial News, 30 April, 5 July, 9 July 1879.

Perth Gazette, 28 October 1848; 4 January 1850; 9 May 1877; 30 April, 9 July, 23 July 1879.

WA Times, 6 April, 23 June 1877; 8 July 1879.

Weekend Australian, 16–17 February 2002 ('Blue, Brown … and Grey').

Weekend Australian Magazine, 2–3 March 2002 ('Dark Secrets …').

West Australian, 23 October 1993 ('Sandgropers stir …'); 30 August 1997 ('Land as Timeless…').

Also by Kim Scott

'*Benang* is brilliant. It is a mature, complex, sweeping historical novel which will remind people of Rushdie, Carey and Grenville at their best. This is an absolute page turner and in the end we are left with a sense of joy and gratitude that such stories are still possible — that the silence has been broken.'
— *Sydney Morning Herald*

'… *Benang* soars to the level of superb storytelling with an emotional punch to the guts, not unlike Toni Morrison's *Beloved*.'
— *Weekend Australian*

Available from www.fremantlepress.com.au
and all good bookstores.

Also by Kim Scott

Billy is drifting, looking for a place to land. A young school teacher, he arrives in Australia's remote far north in search of his own history, his Aboriginality, and his future. He finds himself in a region of abundance and beauty but also of conflict, dispossession and dislocation. On the desperate frontier between cultures, Billy must find his place of belonging.

'*True Country*, Kim Scott's first novel, is superb'
— *Sydney Morning Herald*

'… a superb novel, original in conception and wonderfully evocative'
— *The Australian*

Available from www.fremantlepress.com.au
and all good bookstores.

This edition first published 2013 by
FREMANTLE PRESS
25 Quarry Street, Fremantle 6160
(PO Box 158, North Fremantle 6159)
Western Australia
www.fremantlepress.com.au

First edition published 2005 by Fremantle Press.
Also available as an ebook.

Consultant Editor Janet Blagg
Cover Designer Ally Crimp
Cover image by Frances Andrijich
Printed by Everbest Printing Company, China

National Library of Australia
Cataloguing-in-Publication entry

Scott, Kim, 1957–

Kayang & me / Kim Scott and Hazel Brown.

2nd ed.

ISBN 9781922089229 (pbk)

Nyunga (Australian people)—History.
South-West (W.A.)—History.

Brown, Hazel.

305.89915

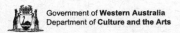

Government of **Western Australia**
Department of **Culture and the Arts**   lotterywest